For God so loved the world, that he gave his only Son, that whoever believes in him should not perish but have eternal life.

John 3:16

The CHILDREN'S BIBLE
in colour

The Children's Bible in Colour
© 2020 North Parade Publishing,
Written by Janice Emmerson
Illustrations by QBS Learning

Published by North Parade Publishing, Bath BA1 1LF, United Kingdom

All rights are reserved. No part of this publication may be reproduced, stored in a retrieval system or transmitted in any form or by any means, electronic, mechanical, photocopying, recording or otherwise, without the prior permission of the Publisher

Printed in China

The CHILDREN'S BIBLE *in colour*

favourite stories from the Bible
retold for children

Contents

The Old Testament

In the Beginning — 14
Genesis 1–2

The Forbidden Fruit — 22
Genesis 3

The First Murder — 28
Genesis 4

Noah and the Big Boat — 30
Genesis 6–7

The Rain Comes — 36
Genesis 7–8

The Wonderful Promise — 42
Genesis 9

Sky High — 44
Genesis 11

Father of a Nation — 48
Genesis 12, 15, 18, 21

The Terrible Test — 52
Genesis 22

The Bowl of Stew — 56
Genesis 25

The Stolen Blessing — 60
Genesis 27

Stairway to Heaven — 64
Genesis 28

Working for Love — 66
Genesis 29

The Dreamer — 70
Genesis 37

Sold For Silver — 74
Genesis 37

The Slave With a Talent — 76
Genesis 39–40

Pharaoh's Dream — 80
Genesis 41

The Begging Brothers — 86
Genesis 42–7

Baby in a Basket — 92
Exodus 1–2

A Dangerous Mission — 96
Exodus 2–7

Plagues! — 100
Exodus 7–10

The Terrible Night — 110
Exodus 11–12

A Path Through the Sea — 114
Exodus 13–15

Food and Water — 120
Exodus 16–17

The Special Rules — 122
Exodus 19–20

The Golden Calf — 124
Exodus 32-3

The Twelve Spies — 126
Numbers 13–14

Crossing the River — 132
Joshua 5

The Walls of Jericho — 136
Joshua 6

The Moon and Sun Stand Still — 140
Joshua 10

Two Brave Women — 142
Judges 4

Three Hundred Men 146
Judges 7

A Loyal Daughter-in-Law 152
Ruth 1–4

Samson the Strong 158
Judges 13, 16

A Voice in the Night 166
1 Samuel 3

The Shepherd Boy 168
1 Samuel 16

A Stone in a Sling 172
1 Samuel 17

The Secret Signal 180
1 Samuel 18-19

The Shepherd King 184
1 Samuel 31; 2 Samuel 1–5

Solomon the Wise 188
1 Kings 3

The Special Temple 192
1 Kings 5–8

Elijah and the Ravens 194
1 Kings 17

Elijah and the Widow 196
1 Kings 17

Battle of the Prophets 200
1 Kings 18

The Chariot of Fire 206
2 Kings 2

The Amazing Jar of Oil 208
2 Kings 2

Washed Clean 210
2 Kings 5

The Power of Prayer 214
2 Kings 18–19

The Potter and His Clay — 218
Jeremiah 18

Conquered! — 220
Jeremiah 29; 2 Kings 25

The Valley of Bones — 222
Ezekiel 37

The Daniel Diet — 226
Daniel 1

The Mysterious Dream — 228
Daniel 2

The Fiery Furnace — 232
Daniel 3

Daniel and the Lions — 238
Daniel 6

Rebuilding Jerusalem — 246
Ezra 1–5; Nehemiah 1-4

Starting Over — 254
Nehemiah 8

The Beauty Contest — 256
Esther 1-2

Enemy of the People — 260
Esther 3

The Brave Queen — 264
Esther 4–8

Saved! — 272
Esther 9

Jonah and the Very Big Fish — 274
Jonah 1–2

A Messenger is Coming — 282
Malachi 1–4

The New Testament

A Visit by an Angel … 284
from Luke 1

An Important Journey … 286
from Luke 2

The Very First Visitors … 292
from Matthew 2 and Luke 2

Following a Star … 296
from Matthew 2

Cousin John … 300
from Matthew 3, Mark 1 and Luke 3

The Big Test … 304
from Matthew 4, Mark 1 and Luke 4

Jesus' Special Friends … 308
from Matthew 4, 9, Mark 1–2 and Luke 5

Water into Wine … 314
from John 2

The Healer … 316
from Matthew 8–9, Mark 1–2 and Luke 5

The Sermon on the Mount … 320
from Matthew 5–7 and Luke 6 and 11–12

The Man Who Amazed Jesus … 328
from Matthew 8 and Luke 7

Jesus Calms the Storm … 330
from Matthew 8, Mark 4 and Luke 8

Just Sleeping … 334
from Matthew 9 and Luke 8

Special Stories … 340
from Matthew 13, Mark 4 and Luke 8

The Mustard Seed and the Yeast … 346
from Matthew 13, Mark 4 and Luke 13

Hidden Treasure — 348
from Matthew 13

A Lamp on a Stand — 350
from Mark 4 and Luke 8 and 11

Five Loaves of Bread and Two Fish — 352
from Matthew 14, Mark 6, Luke 9 and John 6

Walking on Water — 356
from Matthew 14, Mark 6 and John 6

On the Mountain Top — 360
from Matthew 17, Mark 9 and Luke 9

The Frantic Father — 362
from Matthew 17, Mark 9 and Luke 9

The Good Neighbour — 366
from Luke 10

The Rich Fool — 372
from Luke 12

Be Ready! — 374
from Luke 12

The Wise and Foolish Girls — 376
from Matthew 25

The Useless Fig Tree — 380
from Luke 13

The Great Banquet — 382
from Matthew 22 and Luke 14

"I Forgive You (seventy-seven times)!" — 386
from Matthew 18

Lost and Found — 390
from Matthew 18 and Luke 15

The Lost Son — 394
from Luke 15

The Rich Man and the Beggar — 400
from Luke 16

The Grateful Leper — 404
from Luke 17

The Humble and the Proud — 406
from Luke 18

Bags of Gold — 408
from Matthew 25 and Luke 19

The Last Will Be First — 410
from Matthew 20

The Wicked Tenants — 414
from Matthew 21, Mark 12 and Luke 20

Jesus and the Children — 418
from Matthew 19, Mark 10 and Luke 18

Zacchaeus Up a Tree — 422
from Luke 19

Martha and Mary — 426
from Luke 10

Lazarus Lives! — 428
from John 11

The Expensive Perfume — 432
from John 12

Jesus Enters Jerusalem — 434
from Matthew 20–21, Mark 11, Luke 19 and John 12

Troublemaker — 438
from Matthew 22, Mark 12 and Luke 20

Two Small Coins — 442
from Mark 12 and Luke 21

Like a Servant — 444
from Matthew 26, Mark 14, Luke 22 and John 13–15

Betrayed with a Kiss — 450
from Matthew 26, Mark 14, Luke 22 and John 17–18

A Cock Crows — 456
from Matthew 26, Mark 14, Luke 22 and John 18

Pilate Washes his Hands — 458
from Matthew 27, Mark 15, Luke 23 and John 18

A Shadow Falls — 462
from Matthew 27, Mark 15, Luke 23 and John 19

The Empty Tomb — 470
from Matthew 28, Mark 16, Luke 24 and John 20

Alive! — 474
from Luke 24 and John 20

The Ascension — 478
from Mark 16, Luke 24 and Acts 1

Flames of Fire — 480
from Acts 2

Getting Into Trouble . . . and Out Again! — 486
from Acts 3–5

Saul Sees the Light — 494
from Acts 8–9

The Sheet of Animals — 500
from Acts 10

Spreading the Good News — 504
from Acts 13–16 and 20–26

Shipwrecked! — 510
from Acts 27

Letters of Love — 516
from Acts 28, Romans 8, Galatians and 1 Corinthians 12–13

Put on God's Armour! — 522
from Ephesians 6

God is Love — 524
from James, 1 & 2 Peter and 1 John

"I'm Coming Soon!" — 526
from the Book of Revelation

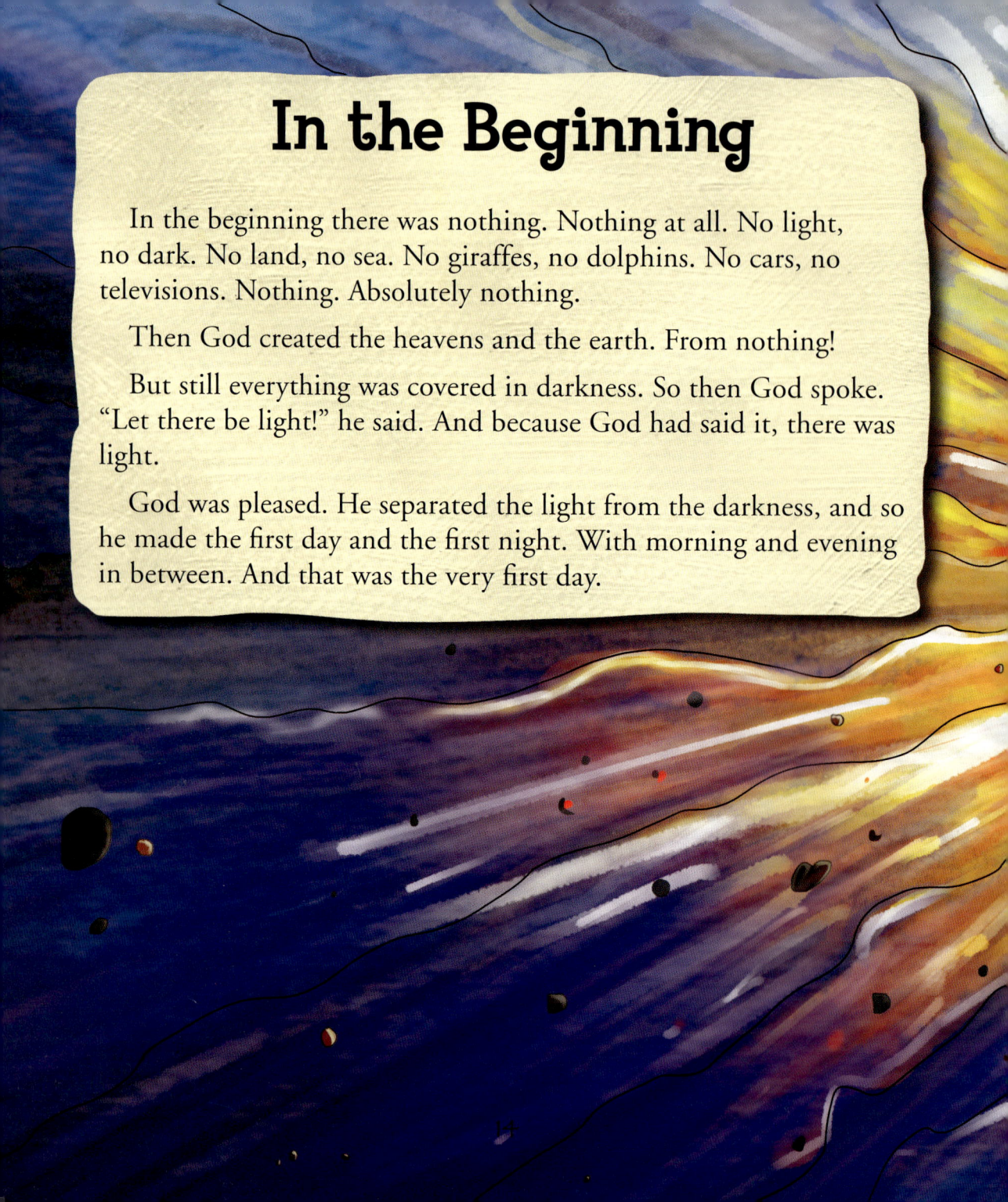

In the Beginning

In the beginning there was nothing. Nothing at all. No light, no dark. No land, no sea. No giraffes, no dolphins. No cars, no televisions. Nothing. Absolutely nothing.

Then God created the heavens and the earth. From nothing!

But still everything was covered in darkness. So then God spoke. "Let there be light!" he said. And because God had said it, there was light.

God was pleased. He separated the light from the darkness, and so he made the first day and the first night. With morning and evening in between. And that was the very first day.

Then God separated the water into two parts, and in between them he made the sky. That was the second day.

On the third day God separated the water from the dry land, and he named the dry land "earth", and the water that was gathered together "seas". And from the earth grew many plants. Soft green grass, and rippling fields of corn, and tall, towering oak trees. And God was pleased.

On the fourth day God chose to put wonderful lights in the sky—the fiery life-giving sun, the cool mysterious moon, and all the bright winking stars that shine when everything else is dark.

On the fifth day God filled the waters with huge sea animals and little fishes and wobbly jellyfish, and in the sky he placed all sorts of birds, from colourful parrots and curious robins, to proud eagles and sleepy owls.

On the sixth day God made animals of all shapes and sizes to slither and crawl and leap and run upon the earth. He made slinking snakes, and jumping frogs, lumbering elephants, and fleet cheetahs.

Then God made something else. Something very special. He made the very first people. He made them in his own image, to look like him. First he made a man, Adam, and then, to be his companion, he made the first woman, Eve. He showed them this wonderful world that he had made and told them to look after it.

And God was pleased with all he had done.

Everything was finished, just as God had planned. And so, on the seventh day, God took some time out. He made this a special day—a holy day. A day to stop and rest and think about things.

The Forbidden Fruit

Everything was going swimmingly. In the midst of this wonderful world that God had created, he had made an extra special place for Adam and Eve to live—a beautiful garden filled with fruit-laden trees, so that they might never go hungry. Juicy oranges, ripe plums, sweet pears—all at their fingertips. God only gave them one rule—they were not to eat the fruit of the Tree of Knowledge that he had planted in the middle of the garden. All the other trees were theirs to enjoy.

So there really shouldn't have been a problem. But the snake had other ideas. The snake was the most cunning of all the animals that God had created. He slithered up to Eve one day and hissed, "Isssss it really true that God has forbidden you to eat from the Tree of Knowledge?"

"Well, yes," replied Eve. "He told us not even to touch it or we would die."

"Sssss!" hissed the wicked snake. "The fruit will make you wise like him. That's the only reason he doesn't want you to eat it! But see how tasty and delicious it looks! It really won't harm you. I promissssse!"

And so the beautiful story that God had started was spoiled. For foolish Eve looked at the luscious fruit and gave way to temptation. She took a bite, and gave some to Adam, and he too ate from the forbidden tree.

In that instance everything changed. Adam and Eve felt different. Everything felt different. Apart from anything else, they both realised at exactly the same time that they were naked. They were wearing nothing at all! Five minutes ago that hadn't been a problem, but now they felt embarrassed and ashamed, and slunk away among the plants to hide.

And when God called down to them, he found them still hiding, and cowering in the shadows. "What have you done?" he said. But he knew. He knew what they had done, and he knew that nothing could be the same from now on.

In anger God cursed the snake to crawl on its belly for the rest of its life, and with a heart filled with disappointment, he told Adam and Eve that from now on they would have to work for their food. No longer would it just drop into their hands. They would have to work the land, and battle against weeds and thorns.

Then he sadly banished Adam and Eve from the beautiful garden and sent them out into the world, clothed in animal skins that he made for them. And at the entrance to the garden he placed an angel with a flaming sword to stand guard.

The First Murder

The years passed by. Adam and Eve now had two sons—Cain, who was a farmer who worked in the fields, and Abel, a shepherd.

One day, both brothers brought offerings to God. Cain brought some of the food that he had grown, while his brother brought the finest meat that he could, from his best lamb. Abel wanted to offer God the very best that he had.

When God accepted his brother's offering and not his, Cain was furious. More than furious, in fact. He felt hurt, and jealous, and bitter, and inside he was burning up with anger.

He asked his brother to go for a walk with him in the fields, and while they were out there alone, Cain struck Abel and knocked him to the ground and killed him.

Later that day, God asked Cain where his brother was.

"How should I know?" asked Cain rudely. "Is it my job to look after my brother?"

God was sad and angry. He knew exactly what had happened, and he could see that Cain wasn't at all sorry for what he had done.

He told Cain that he would never have a permanent home, and sent him away from his family to wander from place to place.

Noah and the Big Boat

More years passed. The land became filled with more and more people. And those people did bad things.

It broke God's heart. He had made such a beautiful world for humans, and they had become so wicked. He wished he had never made them. In fact, he decided to wash his world clean and start all over again.

But there was one man on earth who was good. One man who *did* love and obey God. His name was Noah, and he had three sons—Shem, Ham and Japheth.

God spoke to Noah. He told him that he was "I'm going to send a great flood," he told him. "I am going to wash all the wicked people off the face of the earth. But I want you to build a big boat for yourself and your family. In fact, it will have to be very big, because I want you to gather two of every kind of creature on the earth, one male and one female. Every bird, every animal, everything that creeps or crawls. And you will have to leave enough room for plenty of food!"

This was a strange request. It wasn't even raining. And Noah was probably nowhere close to the sea. But Noah trusted in God. If God told him that this was what he must do, then this was what he would do. It didn't matter if anyone else laughed at him, or made fun of him. Noah was building a boat.

And build a boat he did. With the help of his sons and with a lot of hard work, the boat was finally finished.

And when the boat was finished God told Noah to gather together his family and all the animals, for in just seven days the rain was going to begin.

The Rain Comes

Sure enough, in seven days the clouds grew dark and heavy and the first raindrops fell. Maybe to begin with people were quite pleased. Maybe they needed rain for their crops. But it kept raining. Now it wouldn't have been so pleasant, with the sky dark and ominous, and the ground turned to mud. And on it rained. The rivers burst their banks, the water came up from underground springs, and everywhere you looked there was water. And on it rained. The rooftops weren't safe. People made for the hills. But still it rained. Now the hills were underwater and even the mountains weren't safe.

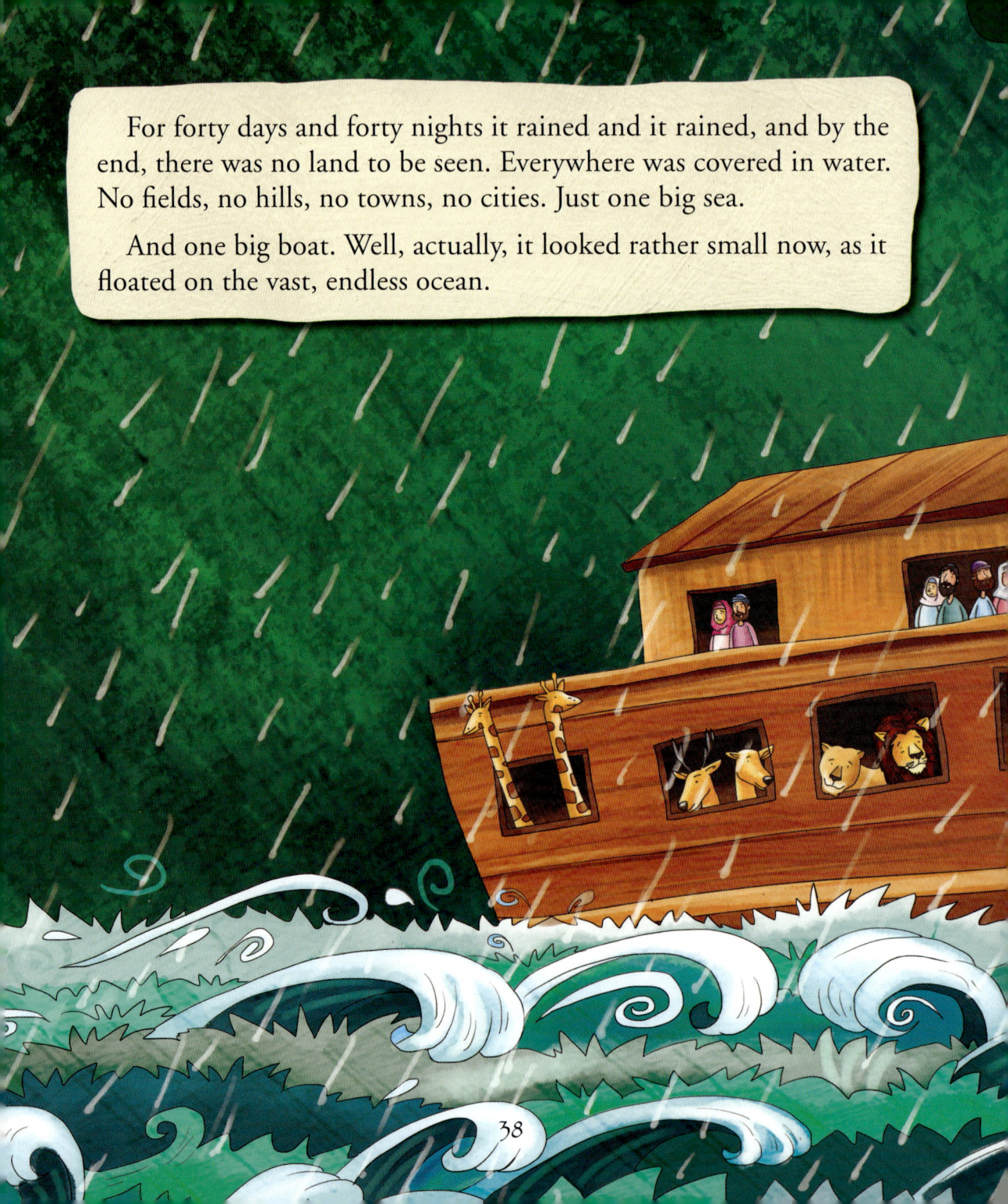

For forty days and forty nights it rained and it rained, and by the end, there was no land to be seen. Everywhere was covered in water. No fields, no hills, no towns, no cities. Just one big sea.

And one big boat. Well, actually, it looked rather small now, as it floated on the vast, endless ocean.

But Noah and his family were safe, just as God had promised. For many months they lived onboard that boat. For another 150 days the world was covered in water. But at the end of that time God sent a wind to blow over the earth, and slowly, slowly, the water began to recede.

At last the boat touched land—the top of a mountain range! After a while Noah sent out a raven, and then a dove, to see if they could find dry land. But the dove flew back, for it could find nowhere to land. A week later, he sent it out again. Again it flew back, but this time it held an olive leaf in its beak. How exciting that must have been!

After another week had passed, Noah sent the dove out yet again. And this time it didn't return! Noah knew that this meant the time had come for him and his family and all the animals to finally leave the boat and start a new life on God's spring-cleaned world.

The Wonderful Promise

God promised to never again send such a dreadful flood, and to show Noah that he meant what he said (which God always does) he placed a beautiful rainbow in the sky. "Whenever I see this rainbow," God told Noah, "I will remember the promise that I made to you and every living creature on this earth."

Sky High

Time passed. To begin with there was only one language on earth. There were many, many people now, for Noah's sons had had children of their own, and they had had children of their own, and so on, and so on … but everyone could understand everyone else because they all spoke the same language.

There came a time when some of Noah's descendants decided to settle down and build a permanent place to live. They planned to build a wonderful city, the crowning glory of which would be a magnificent tower, that reached up into the very clouds. "Then everyone will come from miles around to see," they boasted to one another. "We will be famous!"

And so work started on the tower, and brick by brick it began to rise out of the ground, and higher and higher. And the people were very pleased with themselves.

God looked down upon the city and the tower. He was not happy. They were becoming proud and vain. They had forgotten all about God!

"They think they can do anything because they all speak the same language," said God to himself. "We'll see about that!"

And all at once the city was filled with noise. And it really was just noise. You see, all of a sudden all the people were speaking in different languages. It all sounded like gobbledygook! Gibberish! They were speaking in Ancient Greek and Latin and Arabic and Hebrew and who knew what else? (Well, God knew, obviously).

And work stopped. Well, you see, no one could understand anyone else, so it made it rather difficult to get anything done. After a while they all wandered off in different directions, and were scattered across the earth. Along with their languages.

And the tower became known as the Tower of Babel.

Father of a Nation

Abraham was a good man. Like Noah before him, he trusted in God with all of his heart. So when God told him to pack up all his stuff, gather his wife Sarah, his nephew, and his servants, leave everything that he knew, and head to Canaan, well, that is exactly what he did. And in return for Abraham's trust and love and obedience, God promised to bless him.

Abraham loved God, but he was sad. He and his wife Sarah were old, and they had no children. But one night Abraham had a vision. God led him outside and showed him the sky. "Look at all the stars," God said. "You cannot begin to count them. Your family will be like that. So many that you can't count!"

And God promised Abraham something else, too. He promised him that his descendants would one day own the land of Canaan, the land between the River of Egypt and the great River Euphrates.

But still time passed. Sarah grew very old and still she had no child.

One day she was sitting inside the tent she heard voices outside. Three strangers had appeared, and Abraham had brought them food and water while they rested beneath the shady branches of a tree.

She could hear their voices quite clearly. One of them said to her husband, "Where is Sarah?"

Sarah started at the sound of her name, and heard Abraham tell his guest that she was inside the tent.

The stranger replied, "In a year I will be back. And I promise you that your wife will have a child by then!"

Sarah laughed. She couldn't help herself. Look at how old she was! She couldn't possibly have a child. The idea was ridiculous!

"Why is Sarah laughing?" came the voice. "Nothing is impossible for God!"

And do you know what? Just as the stranger had promised—when Sarah was 90 years old!—she finally had the much-longed for son.

They named him Isaac, which comes from the Hebrew word for "laughter".

"How happy God has made me!" said Sarah, laughing this time with joy and gratitude.

The Terrible Test

Abraham and Sarah loved Isaac dearly. They had waited for a child for so long, and now they had a son they loved him to bits.

But God had one final test that he needed Abraham to pass. It could hardly have been bigger. Abraham's heart sank when he learned what God needed him to do. God wanted him to offer his beloved son as a sacrifice!

Abraham loved Isaac. But he loved God above everything. And he trusted God. His heart was breaking and his steps were heavy, but he saddled his donkey, cut the wood for the sacrifice, and travelled with Isaac to the place he had been told to go.

He put the wood on his son's back, and they climbed to where he was to make the sacrifice.

"Where is the lamb, Father?" asked Isaac questioningly. "I can see the wood, and the fire, but where is the lamb for the sacrifice?"

"God will provide it," said Abraham in a low voice. And then he asked his son to lie down on the altar.

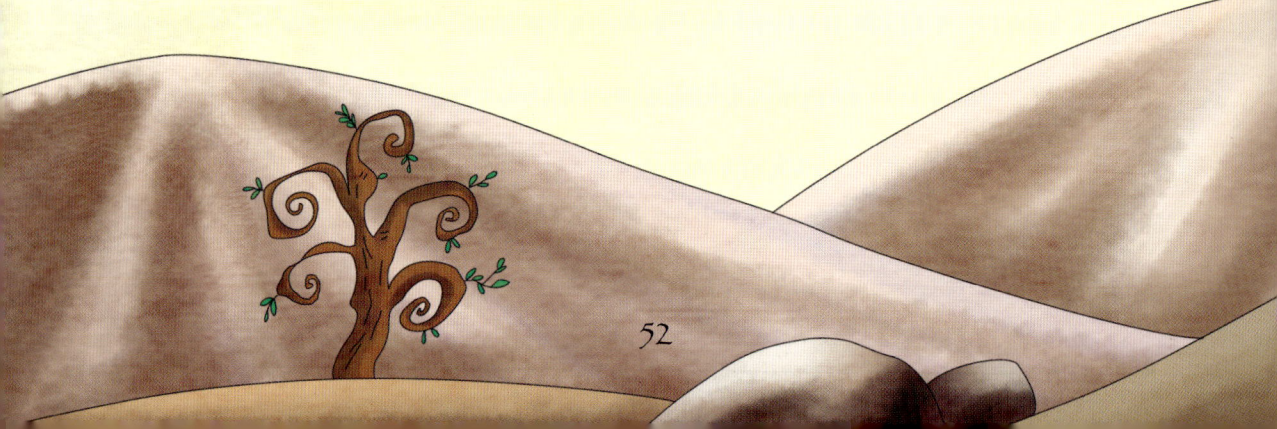

Isaac couldn't understand what Abraham was asking him to do, but he trusted his father, and so he did as he was told without protest.

With a heavy heart, Abraham took the knife in his hand—

—and suddenly an angel spoke to him!

"Abraham, Abraham, put down the knife! Don't harm your son. God knows now that you would do anything he asks of you. He knows that you love him with all your heart, for you were willing to give up your beloved son."

And when Abraham turned around he saw a ram caught in the bushes nearby. God had indeed provided the sacrifice. And with tear-filled eyes, Abraham took his son in his arms and held him close.

God promised Abraham, "Since you were prepared to do this for me, I will bless you and your family. You will have as many descendants as there are stars in the sky. As there are grains of sand on the seashore! Every nation on earth will be blessed through your children, and your children's children. Because you obeyed me!"

God never asks too much of us. And if we love him and trust him and obey him, he will be with us always and forever. There is nothing he would not do for us. He sent a ram to take Isaac's place as a sacrifice. And many, many years later, he would send another sacrifice to take our place. This time, he would send the most precious Lamb of all.

The Bowl of Stew

Jacob was Abraham's grandson. His father was Isaac, and his mother was Rebecca. And he had a twin brother, Esau. Esau was born just seconds before Jacob. But because he had been born first, he was going to inherit his father's role as head of the family. And his share of the inheritance would be twice as large as Jacob's. And his father's blessing would go to him. You see, minutes really do count!

But Esau lost his rights as the firstborn son. In fact, he gave them away. And this is how it happened.

Esau was a hunter. He was his father's favourite (Isaac was very partial to meat!), and he spent his days out looking for game. Jacob preferred to stay closer to home. He was very close to his mother and he held a special place in her heart.

One day Jacob was busy making a delicious stew from some beans, when his brother Esau returned, tired and grumpy, after a long day out hunting.

"I'm starving," complained Esau, moodily. "Give me some of that stew that you have there. It smells great."

"You can have as much stew as you want, if you just agree to give me your rights as the firstborn son," said Jacob craftily, knowing that patience was not his brother's strongest suit.

"Seriously?" asked Esau. "You want me to give up my inheritance for some lousy stew?"

But Esau was very, very hungry. And the stew wasn't lousy at all. In fact, it smelt very, very tasty.

"What use is my inheritance going to be if I starve to death first?" grumbled Esau. "Go on then. Have it your way," and he made sure he took an extra large helping from the pot. That was how much he cared about his rights as firstborn son!

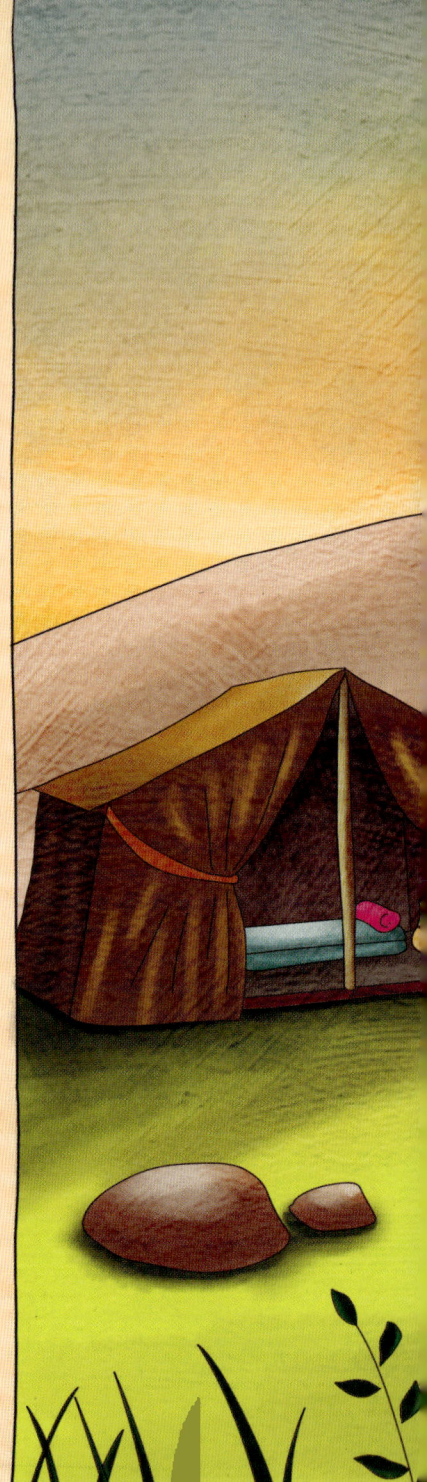

The Stolen Blessing

Some time after that, Jacob managed to cheat his brother out of his father's blessing, too. By now, Isaac was very old indeed and almost completely blind. One day he called to Esau to go hunting and make him a meal of his favourite meat. "Then I will give you my blessing," he promised. And off Esau went.

Now, Rebecca had been listening, and she had other plans. She wanted the blessing to go to her favourite son, and she knew how to make it happen. She told Jacob to go and fetch two young goats, and she promised to prepare a dish with them, and to cook it just the way that Isaac liked it.

"But Mother," protested Jacob, "I know that Father is blind, but don't you think that he will notice when I bring him the food instead of my brother. You know how hairy Esau is! He's almost like a wild animal! Don't you think Father will spot the difference?"

But Rebecca hushed him, and told him just to go and fetch the goats. She would sort the rest.

When Jacob brought the animals to his mother, Rebecca cooked them in Isaac's favourite recipe, and then she took the skins of the goats and wrapped them around Jacob's arms and on his neck (Esau really must have been hairy!). Next Jacob took the meal that she had prepared, and carried it to his father, pretending to be Esau.

"How did you manage to hunt the animals and make this meal so quickly, son?" asked Isaac, who might have been old, but still had some of his wits about him.

"God sent the animals straight to me," blustered Jacob brazenly.

"Come close," said Isaac. "Let me feel you. Then I will know if it really is you."

And when Jacob came to his bedside, Isaac touched his son's skin. "You sound rather like Jacob," he muttered, feeling rather confused. "But you definitely feel like Esau."

And then, because it is what he had promised, he gave Jacob his blessing.

Of course, when Esau came back he soon found out what had happened. To say that he was not best pleased would be rather an understatement. In fact, Rebecca so feared his anger that she sent Jacob away from home to stay with his uncle, so that he would be safe from his brother's vengeance. But the blessing had been given, and it could not be taken back. Jacob would rule over his brother.

The Stairway to Heaven

Jacob was on his way to his uncle's house. He had been walking all day, and the sun had already set before he found a place to spend the night. He found a sheltered spot, and placed a smooth rock as a pillow for his head. Then he lay down, and fell asleep.

As he slept he had a very strange dream. In his dream he saw a stairway that reached from the ground all the way up into heaven. Angels were walking up and down it.

And then Jacob saw God standing by the stairway. God spoke to him. "I am the Lord, the God of your father Abraham, and of Isaac. I will give the land you are lying on to you and to your children. You will have as many descendants as the particles of dust on the ground, and you will spread east and west, and north and south.

"I am with you and I will watch over you wherever you go. And I will bring you back to this land. I won't leave you until I have done what I have promised!"

When he awoke next morning, Jacob took the rock that he had used as a pillow, and made of it a memorial to God. He named the place Bethel, which means "God's house".

Working for Love

Jacob spent rather a lot of time with his uncle Laban. Far more time than he planned to, actually. Or wanted to.

The thing was, soon after arriving on his uncle's farm, he fell head over heels in love with Laban's youngest daughter, lovely Rachel. Cunning Laban decided to make the most of the situation, and promised his nephew that if he would work for him for a short period—seven years should do it—then he could take Rachel as his bride at the end of that time.

As far as Jacob was concerned, seven years was a small price to pay if he could wed his beloved Rachel afterwards.

The seven years flew by, and after they were over Laban held a huge party and brought his daughter to Jacob to marry. They spent the night together and when Jacob woke up, he was shocked and dismayed to find lying beside him, not Rachel, but her elder sister Leah! Laban had tricked him.

(Now, you might wonder how this could possibly have happened. How on earth did Jacob not realise who he was marrying? But you have to remember that the bride would have been heavily veiled, the party would have been lit by candlelight and, of course, Jacob had no idea that his uncle was trying to deceive him so would have suspected nothing.)

Jacob was beside himself. "How could you treat me like this?" he yelled at Laban. "I worked my socks off for you for seven whole years! You knew it was Rachel that I loved! Why did you do this to me?"

Laban stood his ground. "Around here, the younger daughter can't marry before an older daughter. But I'll tell you what—see out the wedding ceremony. That's just one week. And at the end of that time you can take Rachel as your wife, too." (In those days men often had more than one wife.) "But you'll have to work for me for another seven years, of course. I can't be fairer than that!"

Jacob was seething, but what could he do? He loved Rachel with all his heart, and so everything happened just as Laban had wanted. But Jacob was not happy, and he left as soon as he could after his time was up—although even then, Laban tried to cajole and trick him into staying. Jacob was such a good worker!

But what about poor Leah? It was Rachel that Jacob loved, and Leah knew that she was only there on sufferance. But God took pity on her. Jacob might not have loved Leah, but God did, and he sent her many sons and one daughter to console her and look after her. It would be many years before Rachel would have a child …

The Dreamer

Joseph was Jacob's favourite son. Jacob had twelve sons, but he loved none of them as much as he loved Joseph. You see, Joseph had a very special mother—Rachel! It took such a long time for Rachel to fall pregnant that Jacob was old by the time Joseph was born. But that just made him all the more precious.

And to show Joseph just how much he meant to him, Jacob bought him a wonderful coat. It was far finer than anything his brothers had to wear. It was long and colourful, and definitely stood out in the crowd.

Now, Joseph's brothers were—not surprisingly—rather put out by this. It was one thing to know that their father favoured Joseph. It was another thing for him to rub their noses in it. Every time they saw Joseph waltzing around in his fine coat, they grew more and more bitter and jealous and angry.

Jacob hadn't helped the situation. But Joseph made it worse all by himself. You see, Joseph had been given a special gift by God—he had strange dreams. Very strange dreams. And he didn't hesitate to tell his brothers all about them.

"Last night I had a really weird dream. We were all working together in a field, tying the wheat together in stacks. And guess what? My stack stood up, and then yours came and made a ring around it, and all bowed down before it!"

This wasn't the only gem he came up with: "I dreamt that the sun and moon and eleven stars all bowed down before me!" he told them ingenuously.

Telling your brothers that they are going to end up bowing down to you some day possibly isn't the most diplomatic of things to do, especially when you happen to be wearing a super-duper coat that your father has given you.

To be honest, Jacob wasn't that pleased either when his son told him about the dream. "Watch it, young man," he cautioned. "Do you really think that your mother and I and your brothers are going to bow down to you? Don't go getting too big for your boots!"

Sold For Silver

Jacob might have taken the dreams with a pinch of salt—although they did make him wonder—but the brothers were mad. So mad, that they decided to be rid of their irritating brother. One day they were all out in the fields when they decided to throw him down a well and leave him for dead. And that is exactly what they would have done, had they not spied some Ishmaelite traders passing by. Then they came up with the bright idea of selling him as a slave. That way they came away with the princely sum of 20 silver pieces.

The brothers left Joseph with the traders, and then took his precious coat back to their father (but not before tearing it and smearing it with blood).

"Look, Father!" they cried, showing him the coat. "Joseph is lost! Isn't this his coat?"

Jacob was distraught when he saw the spoiled coat. "My son!" he wailed. "He must have been taken by a wild animal!" and he wept and wept. For days. Everyone tried to comfort him, but he said mournfully, "I will be sad about my son until the day I die."

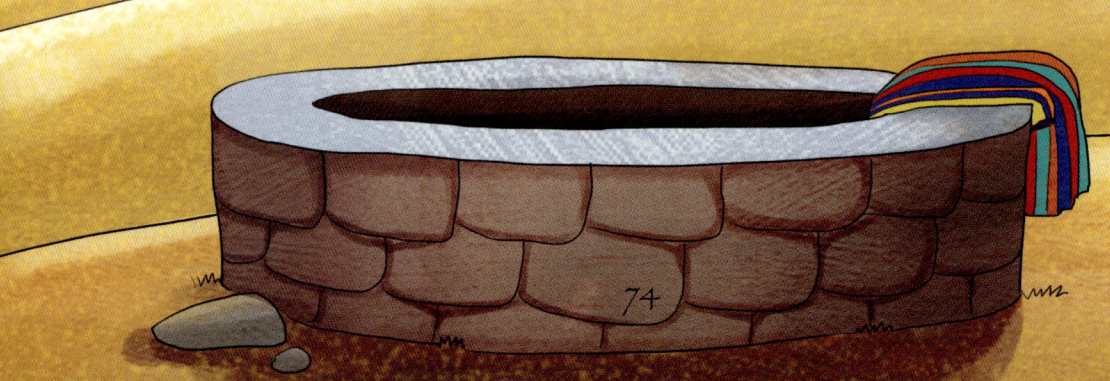

The Slave With a Talent

Joseph was sold by the traders to an important man named Potiphar who worked for mighty Pharaoh, the king of Egypt.

At first things started out pretty well. Potiphar soon discovered that Joseph was a hard worker, and was clever to boot, and he placed Joseph in charge of his household. But that wasn't God's plan. He hadn't sent Joseph to Egypt just to work for Potiphar. And so he threw a spanner in the works.

Now, Joseph was young and strong and handsome, and he soon came to the attention of Potiphar's wife. She wanted to get decidedly friendly with him. Joseph was shocked. "Potiphar trusts me!" he protested. "And anyway, it would be just plain wrong!" And he would have nothing to do with her.

Potiphar's wife was not best pleased. How dare he refuse her! In revenge, she told everyone that Joseph had tried to take advantage of her. As if!

But her husband believed her and was furious. He threw Joseph in jail. And there he stayed.

While Joseph was in prison, two very different men were put in there with him. One was Pharaoh's wine steward. The other was his baker. Both had done something or other to annoy their master, and this was where they ended up.

One morning the men were looking extremely worried. When Joseph asked them what troubled them, they explained that they had both had very strange dreams, and they didn't know what to make of them.

"Tell me your dreams," said Joseph encouragingly. "God will be able to explain them."

The wine steward went first. "In my dream I saw a vine with three branches. They were covered in ripe grapes, so I took them and squeezed them into Pharaoh's cup."

Joseph explained that in three days Pharaoh would pardon him and he would return to work.

At this promising news the baker stepped forward and spoke of his dream. "There were three baskets on top of my head," he said, "and the top one was filled with pastries for Pharaoh. But the birds kept eating them!"

Joseph looked sadly at the baker. "I am sorry," he said, "but in three days Pharaoh will call for your execution!"

Everything happened exactly as Joseph had said. The baker was executed, but the wine steward was pardoned and returned to work for Pharaoh.

Pharaoh's Dream

Time passed, and one night Pharaoh himself had a strange dream. None of his advisers could begin to explain it, and Pharaoh grew troubled and unsettled. It was then that the wine steward remembered about Joseph. When he told his master about him, Pharaoh sent his guards to fetch him immediately.

Joseph stood before Pharaoh in chains. "Explain my dream to me!" demanded Pharaoh.

"I can't do that, Your Majesty," replied Joseph. "But tell me about your dream and God will help me to explain it."

Pharaoh looked at the young Hebrew. He had nothing to lose.

"This is what I dreamed," he began. "I was by the banks of the Nile when out of the river came seven cows. They began eating the grass. They looked strong and healthy. But while I was watching them, seven more cows came up out of the river. These cows were skinny and miserable. But do you know what they did? They gobbled up the fat cows! Every last bit! And when they had eaten them they were just as thin and sickly as they were at the start!

"Then I had another dream. This time I saw seven heads of grain growing on one plant. They were plump and healthy and ripe. But then seven more heads of grain sprouted on the same plant, and these ones were thin and scorched by the wind. And these seven wizened heads of grain gobbled up the seven fat ones!

"So, can your God help me, Joseph? Can you tell me what this is all about?"

Joseph told Pharaoh, "These two dreams are really one and the same. God is sending you a warning. For seven years this land will have healthy crops and bumper harvests. But when that time comes to an end it will be followed by seven hard years of famine!

"Your Majesty," continued Joseph, " you will need to plan well for the famine. Set someone in charge who will collect any extra food and store it for when it is needed. God has sent you these dreams so that you can be ready."

Pharaoh scratched his head for a moment and thought. But to be honest, it was an easy decision. Clearly the man standing right in front of him—slave or not—was the man for the job. Joseph knew what was ahead of them, seemed to have a head for planning, and clearly had God on his side.

And with that, he had his servants fetch Joseph some fine clothes and a special signet ring to show that he was now in charge, second only to Pharaoh himself!

And Joseph didn't let Pharaoh—or God—down. When the bumper harvests that he had forecast came to pass, he made sure that all the farmers put some of the crops aside, and these were gathered up and safely stored in enormous storehouses. So when the dreadful years of famine came, the Egyptians were well prepared. For sure, nothing much grew, apart from a few weeds. But the people had plenty to eat, because so much food had been put aside for this difficult time.

But beyond Egypt it was a different story. Nearby lands had also been hit by the famine, and they had no storehouses full of emergency rations. The people became hungry. Very hungry …

The Begging Brothers

In Canaan Joseph's brothers were among those slowly starving. They heard about the food stores in Egypt, and in the end Jacob decided to send his sons to see if they could buy some grain to see them through the difficult time. But he couldn't bring himself to send all of them. He refused to let his youngest son Benjamin go with his elder brothers. After what had happened to Joseph, Jacob could not bear to lose Benjamin too.

So, ten brothers travelled to Egypt. There they found themselves bowing before a stern prince, hoping desperately that he would sell them some food. Not one of them recognized the man in front of them!

Joseph knew that this was his opportunity to test them. He needed to know if they were sorry for what they had done so many years before. And so he set a trap.

He made them promise to return with their younger brother. Only this way, he said, could he be sure that they were not spies! He filled their bags with grain, and sent them to fetch Benjamin. But he kept one of his brothers, Simeon, in prison, to make sure of their return.

Jacob didn't want to let Benjamin go to Egypt. How he wanted to keep him safe and sound at home! But the grain that the brothers had brought back was used up all too soon. They had no choice but to return and buy some more. And Jacob had no choice but to let Benjamin go with them.

When Joseph saw Benjamin he was so overcome that he had to hide his face. He wanted to do nothing so much as hug him with all his might. But the test was not yet complete. He wined and dined the brothers, then sent them on their way with sacks laden with grain. And in those sacks he also had his servant secretly place the money that they had brought to pay for the grain. And to crown things off, he told his servant to hide his own special silver goblet in young Benjamin's sack. Then off the brothers set, across the desert.

Imagine the horror of the brothers when Egyptian soldiers came after them and stopped them in their tracks. And imagine how they felt when the soldiers opened the sacks and out of Benjamin's sack tumbled the fine silver cup!

The brothers were dragged before Joseph. They fell to their knees and pleaded for his forgiveness. They told him that they knew now that God was punishing them for something wicked that they had done long ago. Joseph said that he would set them all free—all apart from Benjamin, that is! Benjamin would stay to be his slave!

The brothers wept in horror. Then Judah stepped forward. "Your highness," he said in desperation. "Please let the boy return home! I beg you! It will break our father's heart if he loses Benjamin. Take me instead! I promised to bring him back safely. Please take me!"

Joseph could not stop the tears from running down his face. He sent his servants away, and was alone with his brothers.

"Can you not see that it is me?" he wept. "Your brother Joseph?"

The brothers could hardly believe their ears. They didn't know what to think. They were overwhelmed with joy and confusion and more than a little fear! What would he do to them? He certainly had the right to punish them!

But Joseph hugged his brothers to him. "Don't worry about the past!" he soothed them. "It was all God's plan. Everything you did was what God wanted to happen. He sent me here so I could save you!"

When Pharaoh learned the news he was almost as excited as Joseph was! He told Joseph to send his brothers to fetch their father and their families and bring them to Egypt, where he would give them the finest land to farm. And so Jacob was reunited with his beloved son, and the tears were tears of joy.

Baby in a Basket

Much time had passed since Pharaoh welcomed Jacob and his family to Egypt with open arms. Now the situation was decidedly different. The Egyptians had turned against the Hebrews. They felt that there were too many of them, and that they might join up and pose a threat. The new Pharaoh had turned them into slaves. And even worse, to keep the Hebrew numbers down, his last decree had been to order the death of any newborn Hebrew baby boys!

Miriam was sad and scared. She had a tiny baby brother. He had been born just a couple of months ago, and all that time her mother had kept him hidden from the Egyptian soldiers. They had loved him, and held him and kissed him. But now it was no longer safe to keep him. Miriam's mother had tenderly wrapped her baby in a blanket, and gently placed him in a basket, and left him floating among the swaying reeds that grew on the edge of the Nile River. Maybe someone would find him and look after him! Maybe he would be safe!

And Miriam was watching nervously to see what happened, safely hidden behind some bushes.

Just then, Pharaoh's daughter came down to the river to bathe. Maybe she saw the basket bobbing in the reeds, or maybe she heard the baby babbling, but something drew her to the edge of the water. She told one of her maidservants to bring the basket to her. When she saw the baby boy, her heart went out to it. She knew that it was one of the Hebrew babies, but she wanted to keep it safe.

Miriam stepped out of the shadows and stepped before the princess. "Your Highness," she said bravely, "would you like me to fetch a Hebrew woman to nurse this baby for you?"

The princess smiled at Miriam. "Please do," she replied.

And so it was that Miriam's mother looked after her own baby until he was old enough to go and live in the palace with Pharaoh's daughter. And the princess named the boy Moses, for he had been pulled out of the water.

A Dangerous Mission

The years passed and the boy grew to be a man. Moses was noble and strong, but while he had grown up in a palace with Egyptians all around him, he never forgot his own people. One day when he saw an Egyptian brutally beating a Hebrew slave, he lost his temper and killed him. Now he had to leave Egypt, for it wasn't safe for him to remain.

Moses travelled to Midian, where he spent many years as a humble shepherd. But God had other plans for him. One day Moses was tending his sheep when he noticed a nearby bush on fire! The bush was covered in flames, yet the leaves did not burn! Moses approached the bush filled with curiosity and trepidation. How much more astonished do you imagine he was when he heard God's voice?

"Take your shoes off, Moses," said God, "for this is holy ground. I am the God of your father, of Abraham, of Isaac, and of Jacob.

"I have seen how miserable my people are in Egypt. And I have come to rescue them! I will bring them up out of that land and take them to a land flowing with milk and honey.

"And you will go to Pharaoh and lead my people out of Egypt!"

Moses hid his face in fear. "My Lord," he whispered, "how can I go to Pharaoh? Me? I am no one! You should send someone else!"

"I will be with you, Moses," said God, and he would not take "no" for an answer. But he did agree to send Moses' brother Aaron with him, to help him with the task.

So, all too soon, Moses found himself standing before Pharaoh in his mighty throne room, with his brother Aaron by his side.

"Your majesty," said Moses, trembling, "the God of Israel says that you are to let his people go, so that they can hold a festival in the desert to honour him."

Maybe not surprisingly, Pharaoh's response wasn't particularly positive. It is altogether possible that he laughed at Moses' audacity. Or snorted. Or was just plain angry. Whatever the case, the answer was a resounding "no". Why on earth would he go and give all his slaves a holiday?! Who was this "God" fellow anyway?

Still, Moses and Aaron had a few tricks up their sleeves.

Aaron threw his walking staff down onto the ground, and in an instant it was transformed into a fearsome serpent! Pharaoh looked just a little bit unsettled, but then his magicians huddled together and then they, too, threw their staffs on the ground and they all turned into snakes. Aaron's snake swallowed them all up, but Pharaoh was not impressed. He would not let the Hebrews go.

Plagues!

Now it was time for God to teach Pharaoh a lesson. He was going to send him ten dreadful warnings—in the shape of ten dreadful plagues.

The first plague was really rather horrible. God told Aaron to strike the River Nile with his staff and instantly the water turned to blood. The whole river was red! Yuck! All the fish died. No one could drink from the river. Washing in it was a big no-no. And as for the smell … Well, let's not dwell on that.

God left the river like that for seven whole days. Then he sent Moses to tell Pharaoh that if he didn't free the Hebrews then the whole country would be covered by frogs.

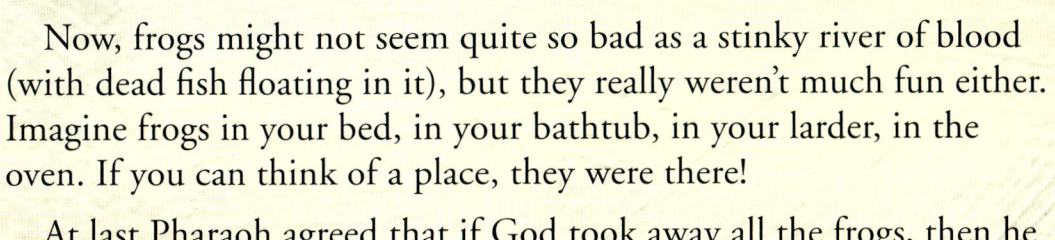

Now, frogs might not seem quite so bad as a stinky river of blood (with dead fish floating in it), but they really weren't much fun either. Imagine frogs in your bed, in your bathtub, in your larder, in the oven. If you can think of a place, they were there!

At last Pharaoh agreed that if God took away all the frogs, then he would let the Hebrews go. But wouldn't you know it? As soon as all the frogs were dead and cleared away, Pharaoh went back on his word. "I've changed my mind," he said. "You can't go!"

Next God sent a plague of gnats. Nasty biting gnats. And everywhere that the frogs had been, the gnats went too. The ground was covered with them. You couldn't move without stepping on at least a dozen of them.

After that came a plague of flies. They filled the air. The skies were dark. Dark with horrid, buzzing flies. Swarms of flies came into Pharaoh's grand palace and into the people's houses (but not those of the Hebrews). If you were trying to eat your dinner you were as likely to swallow a mouthful of flies. Double yuck!

But still Pharaoh wouldn't change his mind.

Then God sent a horrid disease that affected all the animals of the Egyptians. All the horses, and cows, and sheep, and camels, and goats, and hens. And they all died.

But still Pharaoh stood his ground.

Then it was the humans that came under attack. The Egyptians found their skin covered with boils. Itchy, oozing, painful boils. From head to toe. And everywhere in between. They just couldn't stop scratching!

But Pharaoh would not give in.

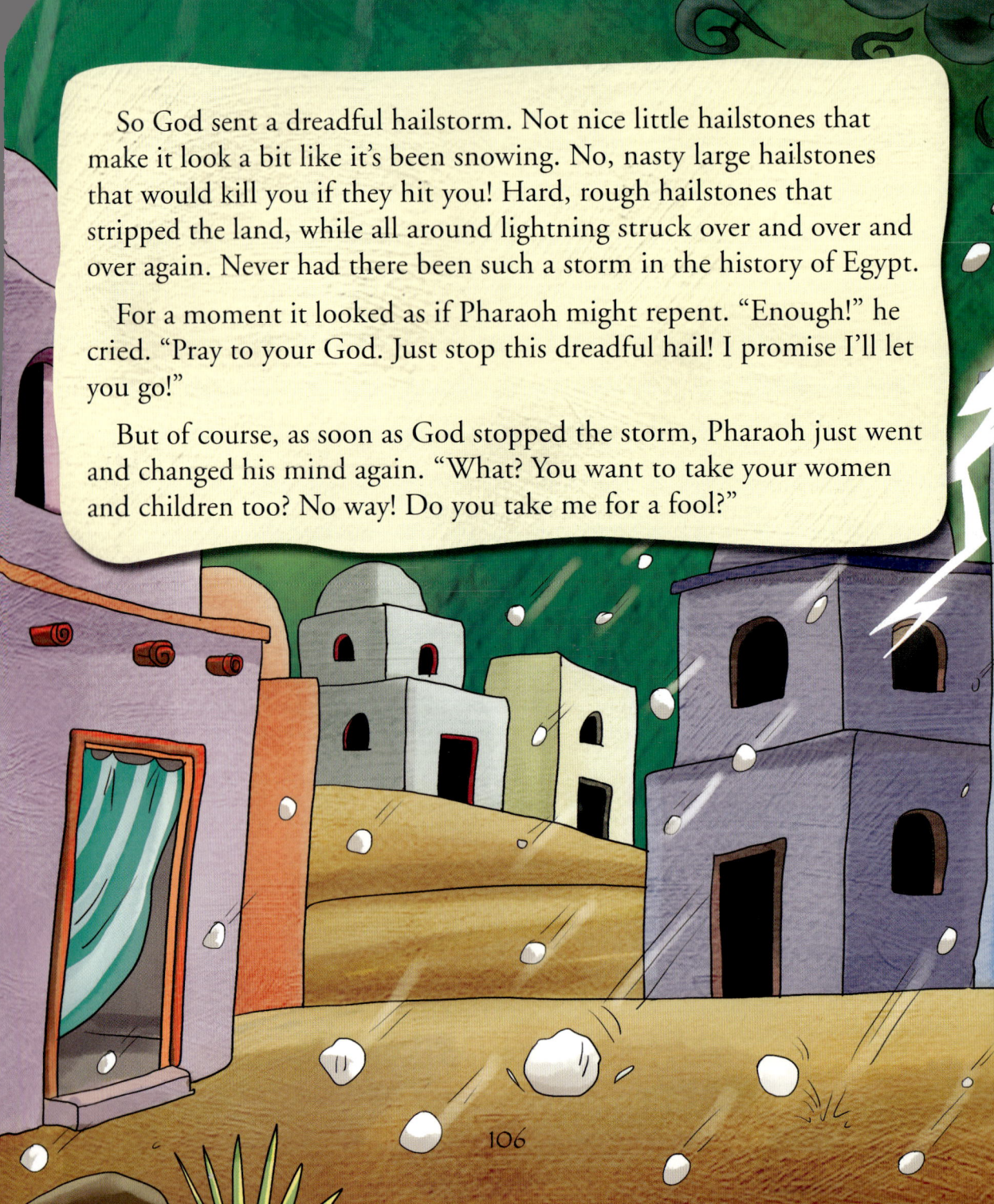

So God sent a dreadful hailstorm. Not nice little hailstones that make it look a bit like it's been snowing. No, nasty large hailstones that would kill you if they hit you! Hard, rough hailstones that stripped the land, while all around lightning struck over and over and over again. Never had there been such a storm in the history of Egypt.

For a moment it looked as if Pharaoh might repent. "Enough!" he cried. "Pray to your God. Just stop this dreadful hail! I promise I'll let you go!"

But of course, as soon as God stopped the storm, Pharaoh just went and changed his mind again. "What? You want to take your women and children too? No way! Do you take me for a fool?"

Next, any plants that were still alive were decimated by a swarm of locusts. Nothing green remained in the whole of the land of Egypt!

But Pharaoh still wouldn't budge.

And then God sent total darkness to cover Egypt for three whole days. Absolute and total darkness. The Egyptians couldn't see one another. They couldn't even see their own hands if they waved them around in front of their faces! No one went outside their front door. They would have got lost!

"Well, maybe you can take your women and children," muttered Pharaoh reluctantly to Moses. (For someone who was probably used to being bathed and dressed and fed and generally waited on hand and foot, this total darkness thing was probably rather inconvenient.) "But you're not taking any of your animals with you! Don't even think about it!"

"We need our animals," said Moses firmly. "We're not leaving a single one behind."

So guess what? Pharaoh put his foot down. "I'm not letting you go!" he screeched. "And get out of my sight! I never want to see you again!"

Moses warned him that the worst was yet to come. But Pharaoh would not listen, and so Moses left.

The Terrible Night

And the worst really was to come. God was going to send the most dreadful plague of all upon wicked Pharaoh and the Egyptians. That night he told Moses that he would pass through the land at midnight, and every firstborn son in Egypt would die, from the son of Pharaoh himself to the son of the prisoner chained to the walls of the dungeon, deep below his palace.

But first God told Moses how the Hebrews could protect themselves. Each household must kill a lamb and wipe the blood on the doorposts of the house. And they were not to step out of the door all night.

And sure enough, it happened just as God had said. When morning came the whole land was filled with the sound of wailing and weeping, for all the firstborn sons were dead. There was not one home where the people were not mourning a death. But not a single one of the Hebrew sons had died, for the Lord had passed over their houses.

Then Pharaoh summoned Moses and Aaron to him. "Go!" he cried. "Go now—right now! And take all your people with you. And all your stupid animals too!"

The Egyptians were desperate to see them go. They gave them silver and gold, and other things too, just to get rid of them. The Hebrews packed in a rush, and soon there was a huge procession of people leaving the country that they had been in for hundreds of years! Now they were on the move again—and this time they were heading to the Promised Land, the wonderful land that God had spoken to Moses about—the land of milk and honey!

A Path Through the Sea

The Hebrews travelled southwards towards the Red Sea. They were on their way to a wonderful new home! God had sent a pillar of cloud each day to guide them and show them where to go, and each night a pillar of fire lit up the sky, so that they could travel by day or by night.

Their hearts were light and full of joy. They were slaves no more. They were leaving Egypt at last. Pharaoh had let them go!

But guess what? Pharaoh had had yet another change of heart. Losing that many slaves in one fell swoop must have been a bit of a blow, or maybe he just needed someone to take his anger out on. Either way, he decided that he would get the Hebrews back, and he set off with his army in swift pursuit.

When the Hebrews saw the clouds of dust in the distance behind them they quickly guessed what had happened. And just as quickly they started panicking. Which was hardly surprising, given that they had just reached the shore of the Red Sea, and the way ahead was barred by the water.

"What have you done?" they cried to Moses in despair. "We shall all be killed! We'd have been better off staying in Egypt than to die here in the desert!"

But Moses was not flustered. He still trusted in God. After all that had happened, why wouldn't he? God had always kept his word. Moses knew that God wouldn't have brought them here just to be killed.

"Calm down," he said to the crowd around him. "Don't be afraid. God is with us. Have faith in him and he will save us."

And then God spoke to Moses and told him to raise his staff and stretch it out over the sea. And when Moses did as God commanded, the waters in front of him parted. All night God drove the sea back with a strong wind, and a wall of water rose up on the right and on the left, leaving a dry path straight ahead. Then the Hebrews travelled across the Red Sea, without getting even a tiny bit wet!

Now, the Egyptians had not clearly seen what had happened (God had sent the cloud of dust behind the Hebrews to hide them), but when they saw the open path across the sea they did not hesitate. All Pharaoh's officers and horsemen and chariots followed hard on the heels of the Hebrews, and as soon as they were all on the path God closed the waters together again, and every last one of them was swallowed up by the sea. Not one of the soldiers survived.

But the people of Israel reached the far side of the Red Sea safe and dry—and free. And there they gave thanks to God for all he had done. They danced and sang and praised God with all their hearts. I imagine that was some party!

Food and Water

As you might imagine, travelling across the desert was never going to be an easy affair. They couldn't possibly carry enough food and water with them and to start with they were terrified that they would starve to death or die of thirst. But God was with them. Whatever they needed, he gave them.

Every morning when they woke up, the ground would be covered with white flakes—like flakes of frost. They tasted like wafers made with honey if they weren't cooked, but could be ground down to make cakes which they could bake. Each morning they gathered just what they needed for the day, except on the day before the Sabbath, when they gathered twice as much. They called these flakes manna from heaven!

And when they needed water and there was no oasis or stream for them to drink from, and the people grew very thirsty and started shouting at Moses and complaining more than ever, then God told Moses to strike a rock with his staff and water gushed out—fresh, cool water in the middle of the desert!

Of course, people being people, they still complained and moaned and grumbled. They were whiny and ungrateful. They were always very quick to speak out about how hard their lives were, and very slow to remember how God had freed them from slavery, brought them across a great sea, and was looking after them in the desert, every single day!

The Special Rules

In time, Moses led the people to Mount Sinai. There God spoke to Moses alone, high up on the mountain slopes. Long ago God had made a special deal, or covenant, with Abraham. He had promised to make him the father of a great nation, and he had promised that these would be his own special people, and he would give them a land to live in. Now God wanted to renew his covenant with the Hebrews. He wanted them to know how much he loved them, and he wanted them to love him above all else in the world and to obey his commands.

There was also something else that God spoke to Moses about. He wanted to give his people a set of rules. These rules would keep them safe. They would help them to get along with one another in peace and harmony, they would help to keep them well and healthy, and they would help to keep them close to God. They were to worship only God, and never pray to any pretend gods. They were to keep his name holy, and to remember what the Sabbath was really for (that seventh day, when God rested and took stock of all he had done).

And there were other rules about not killing, or lying, or stealing, or cheating, or being envious. And they were to respect their parents. There were many more commandments given by God to Moses, covering every aspect of daily life, but these are the most famous.

God wrote his commandments on two stone tablets, which Moses took down to the people.

The Golden Calf

But do you know what? By the time Moses went back down the mountain (he had been up there for quite some) the people had already got into trouble. While Moses had been up the mountain, drawing up the covenant with God and learning all the rules, the people had begun to worry that he might not come back. They had asked Aaron to make them a new god to lead them, and they had given him all their gold jewellery (all the earrings and bracelets and necklaces and rings) and he had put them in a giant pot and melted them down, and had shaped from them a golden calf. He had placed the calf on an altar, and by the time that Moses came back, the people were dancing and singing around the golden calf, praising it and worshipping it.

When Moses realised what they were up to he saw red. He threw the two stone tablets to the ground and they broke into hundreds of pieces. Then he took the golden calf and tossed it in the fire until it melted away. Then he ground it to powder.

God was angry too. He punished the people with a plague. But Moses pleaded with him to forgive them and to stay close to them. And God renewed his covenant with the Hebrews and gave them a new set of stone tablets, and the Hebrews promised to obey him.

They made a special wooden chest to hold the stone tablets in, covered in the purest gold. It was known as the Ark of the Covenant. And they carried this with them, wherever they travelled.

The Twelve Spies

By this time the Hebrews had been in the desert for a couple of years, give or take. Now God told Moses to send some men to check out the new land that he had promised them, the land of Canaan.

Moses chose one man from each of the twelve tribes of Israel (that each came from one of the twelve sons of Jacob), and he sent them out to see what the land was like. What were the towns like? Did the people look weak or strong? Did the soil look good? Was there clean water?

Forty days later they were back . . . laden with juicy grapes, and ripe figs, and rosy pomegranates.

"The land is so green!" they enthused. "Anything seems to grow there!"

Moses smiled. This was great news. It was just as God had promised.

But then some of the spies piped up, "But there's no point in going there. It would be a suicide mission!"

You see, the spies had certainly spotted fine harvests and lush land. But they had also seen fortified towns and cities, and strong men who were much, much bigger than they were!

"We don't stand a chance," said one of the spies. "We'd never be able to attack any of those cities. You should have seen the size of the walls!"

"Yeah," chimed another, "and those people are practically giants!"

Then another of the spies, a man named Caleb, stepped forward and said, "You're cowards! Do you want to stay wandering in the desert for the rest of your lives? We can definitely conquer this land!"

And Joshua came to join him. "The Lord promised us that land. He will be with us. He will lead us into the land—if we just trust in him and obey him!"

But still the Hebrews were scared.

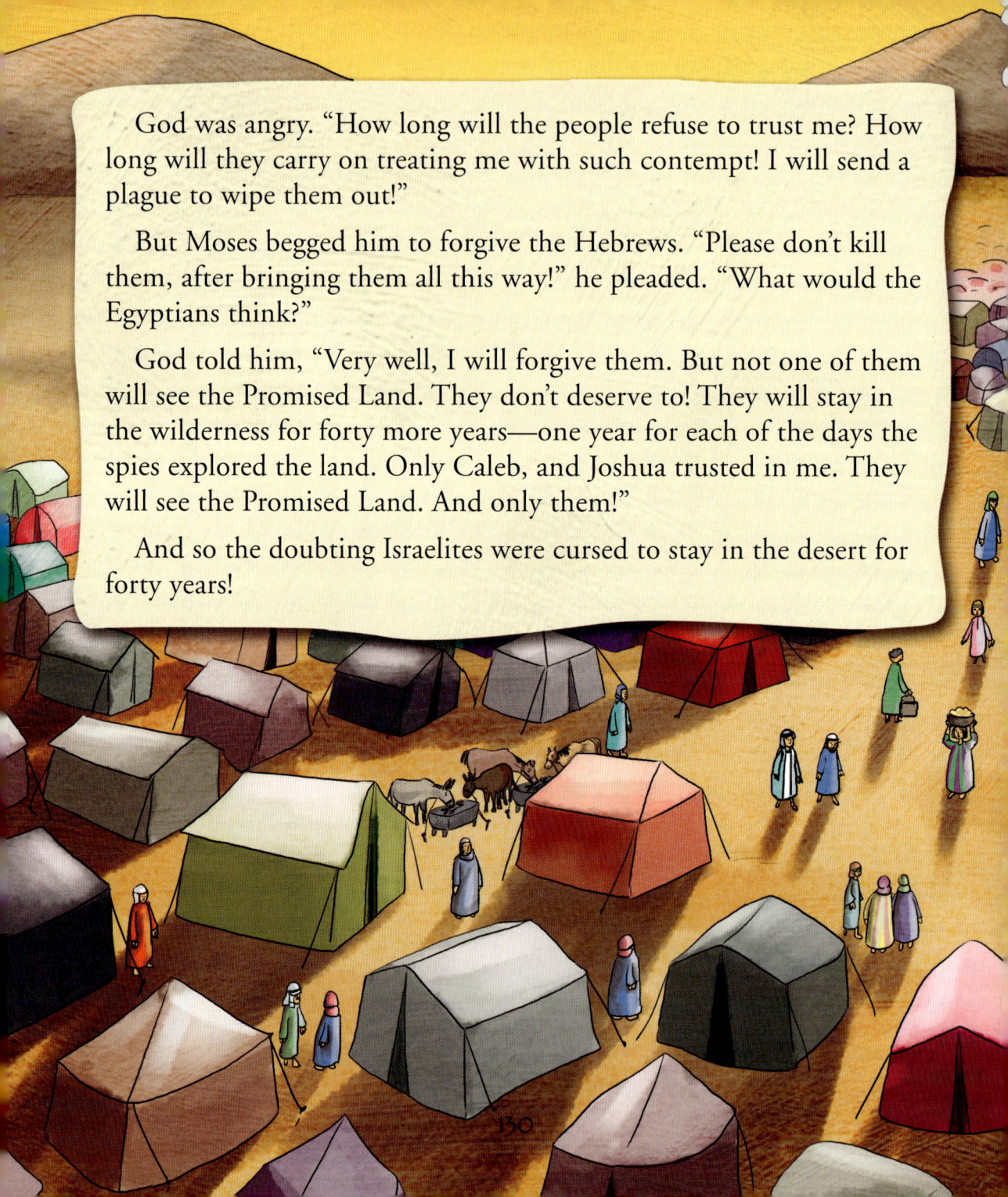

God was angry. "How long will the people refuse to trust me? How long will they carry on treating me with such contempt! I will send a plague to wipe them out!"

But Moses begged him to forgive the Hebrews. "Please don't kill them, after bringing them all this way!" he pleaded. "What would the Egyptians think?"

God told him, "Very well, I will forgive them. But not one of them will see the Promised Land. They don't deserve to! They will stay in the wilderness for forty more years—one year for each of the days the spies explored the land. Only Caleb, and Joshua trusted in me. They will see the Promised Land. And only them!"

And so the doubting Israelites were cursed to stay in the desert for forty years!

Crossing the River

Joshua stood on the banks of the mighty Jordan River. The river was in flood. The white frothy waters rushed passed his feet and roared in his ears. There wasn't a bridge in sight.

And yet today was the day that God had told him to lead the Hebrews into the Promised Land! And Joshua knew better than to doubt God. If God said it would happen, then it would happen.

Moses was no longer with them. He had died—at the ripe old age of one hundred and twenty!—on the slopes of Mount Nebo, overlooking the Promised Land. Now Joshua was the leader of the Israelites, and it was his job to take his people into Canaan.

Joshua told everyone to gather together all their things, and be ready. Then he told the priests to lift up the Ark of the Covenant and to go ahead. Straight ahead—into the river!

As soon as the first toe of the first priest touched the raging river the waters parted. To one side was a huge wall of water, but ahead of them was dry ground! The priests crossed half-way, and then all the Hebrews walked across the riverbed to the other side.

When every last person had crossed the river, Joshua told one man from each of the twelve tribes to take a stone from the middle of the riverbed, where the priests still stood. Then, and only then, did the priests themselves finish crossing the river, and as soon as the last one had stepped safely onto the shore, the river crashed down behind them.

Joshua gathered the twelve stones and made a special monument out of them to remind the Hebrews how God had brought them across the River Jordan.

The Walls of Jericho

Yet another hurdle stood before Joshua and the land that God had promised his people. This time the obstacle took the form of walls—huge walls! The walls of the city of Jericho were thick and strong and tall. And when the people inside had heard that the Hebrews were headed in their direction, they had locked and barred the gates. And thrown away the key!

Now, the people of Jericho were scared. They had heard about these Hebrews and their God—the God who could part seas and rivers, and who could send dreadful plagues. They were cowering on the inside.

But from the outside, it wasn't altogether clear exactly how the Hebrews were going to take the city. They didn't have any siege engines, or any cannons, or even any ladders. However, they did have God!

God told Joshua exactly what he wanted him to do. For six days all the armed Hebrew men marched once around the city. In front of them went seven priests carrying trumpets, ahead of the Ark of the Covenant.

On the seventh day they marched around the city walls seven times. On the last time round the priests sounded a loud blast on their trumpets, and Joshua told all the Hebrews to shout out loudly. And as the soldiers shouted and the priests trumpeted the walls of the city began to quiver and shake, and then the walls collapsed in a cloud of dust!

Then the soldiers charged in and took the city!

And the story of how God had delivered Jericho to the Hebrews was passed throughout the land, and people were afraid.

The Sun and Moon Stand Still

Joshua and his soldiers were fighting against the Amorites. They had come to the rescue of the people of Gibeon who were under attack. And things were going swimmingly.

The Hebrews had marched all through the night and had taken the Amorites by surprise. That was their first advantage. As for their second advantage—well, that was God! The Hebrew soldiers were brave, and fought hard, but it was the huge hailstones that God sent from the heavens that were really doing the damage, and Joshua could see that they were well on the way to winning the battle.

But he could also see that night was approaching fast. The battle would not be over before the sun fell behind the horizon. And no one wanted to fight in the dark. How could you be sure who you were fighting? Was that fellow in front of you the enemy or your best mate?!

Joshua really wanted to get this battle over and done with. There was really only one thing to do.

Joshua looked towards the heavens. "Sun," he shouted loudly, "stand still over Gibeon. And you, moon, stand still over the Valley of Aijalon!"

And the sun stopped in the middle of the sky and the moon stopped too, and the Hebrews kept on fighting the Amorites, and the battle was won! Just because God listened to Joshua!

Two Brave Women

Many years had passed since the Israelites had first stepped foot in Canaan. Now the people were ruled by judges—special leaders who took charge of things in time of trouble. And it was a time of trouble!

The people had forgotten all about their special agreement with God. They had fallen back into wicked ways and had forgotten to trust and obey him. Instead of driving the Canaanites out of the land that God had promised them, the Israelites got friendly with them, and some of them took wives from among them and began to worship their gods and forget about God's laws.

So God had allowed their enemies to fall upon them. King Jabin, and the commander of his armies, General Sisera had taken control of the land. And now the people of Israel remembered about God and begged him to help them!

God took pity on them. He told Deborah what to do.

Deborah had a soldier named Barak gather an army of ten thousand men. She told him that with God's help she was going to deliver Sisera and all his soldiers right into his hands. Deborah trusted God.

But Barak wasn't totally convinced. He knew that the men who had flocked to him were not properly trained, and they didn't have enough weapons. Whereas General Sisera's army had better weapons, better training—and many, many more men!

He reluctantly agreed to lead the army into battle—but only if Deborah went with him! He didn't have faith in God.

The Israelites met Sisera and his chariots on the slopes of Mount Tabor. The ground was a quagmire, and the chariot wheels became stuck fast in the mud, throwing the Canaanite forces into confusion and disarray. The Israelites fell upon their enemy and by the end of the day, not a single enemy soldier was left standing on the battlefield.

The Israelites had won, just as Deborah had promised, but in all the confusion General Sisera had managed to slip away unnoticed, and had returned, wet and angry and dismayed to the army camp, and had made his way to the tent of one of his allies.

There a woman named Jael let him in, and gave him a drink, and told him where he could lie down and rest.

But Jael didn't like Sisera. In fact, she hated him!

As soon as the general fell asleep, she took a tent peg and a hammer and used them to kill him!

When news spread of the death of Sisera, Jael was celebrated and honoured for her bravery and for her role in saving the Israelites from their enemy.

Three Hundred Men

Many years passed. The people turned away from God and fell into wicked ways—no surprise there, really, if we're going to be honest. Heroes had come and gone, and time after time the Hebrews stopped trusting in God and thought they could sort things out themselves.

Now a new enemy threatened them, the Midianites. For seven long years the Hebrews had been terrorized by these new invaders. Many were forced to hide in the hills, in fear of their lives. They called out to God, "Help us!" they begged. "We're sorry!"

God sent them a new hero, a man named Gideon. He wanted Gideon to rescue his people from the Midianites. Gideon wasn't too keen on the job, to begin with. He really wasn't sure he was the right man for the job. But God knew what he was doing.

Gideon gathered a large army. He thought he would need it to defeat their enemies. But God told him he had too many men.

"Send any home who are scared," God told Gideon.

After Gideon had spoken to his army only a third were left! He only had ten thousand men left, but the tents of the Midianites stretched as far as the eye could see. What on earth was God playing at?

"Still too many," said God. "Tell them to go and drink from the river. Send away any who kneel down to drink. Take only those who cup the water in their hands."

Gideon did as he was told. Only three hundred men were left.

Three hundred! How on earth could they possibly defeat the Midianites? There were over a hundred thousand of them!

But God reassured him, "With these three hundred men I will deliver the Midianites into your hands."

Gideon trusted in God, but still, that night as he looked down upon the endless tents of his enemy, he couldn't but help feel the teeniest bit anxious. Well, maybe quite a bit anxious, if he was being truthful.

God knew that he was worried. He told Gideon to creep down to the enemy camp and listen to what they were saying.

Gideon did as he was told, and as he hid in the bushes he overheard two soldiers talking about their dreams. "I had a really horrible dream," said one of them. "I dreamt that a round loaf of bread came rolling down the hill and crashed into my tent and knocked it flat!"

"Oh dear," wailed his companion. "That can only mean one thing! It'll be that dreadful Hebrew soldier. What's his name? Gideon! God must have given the whole camp to him!"

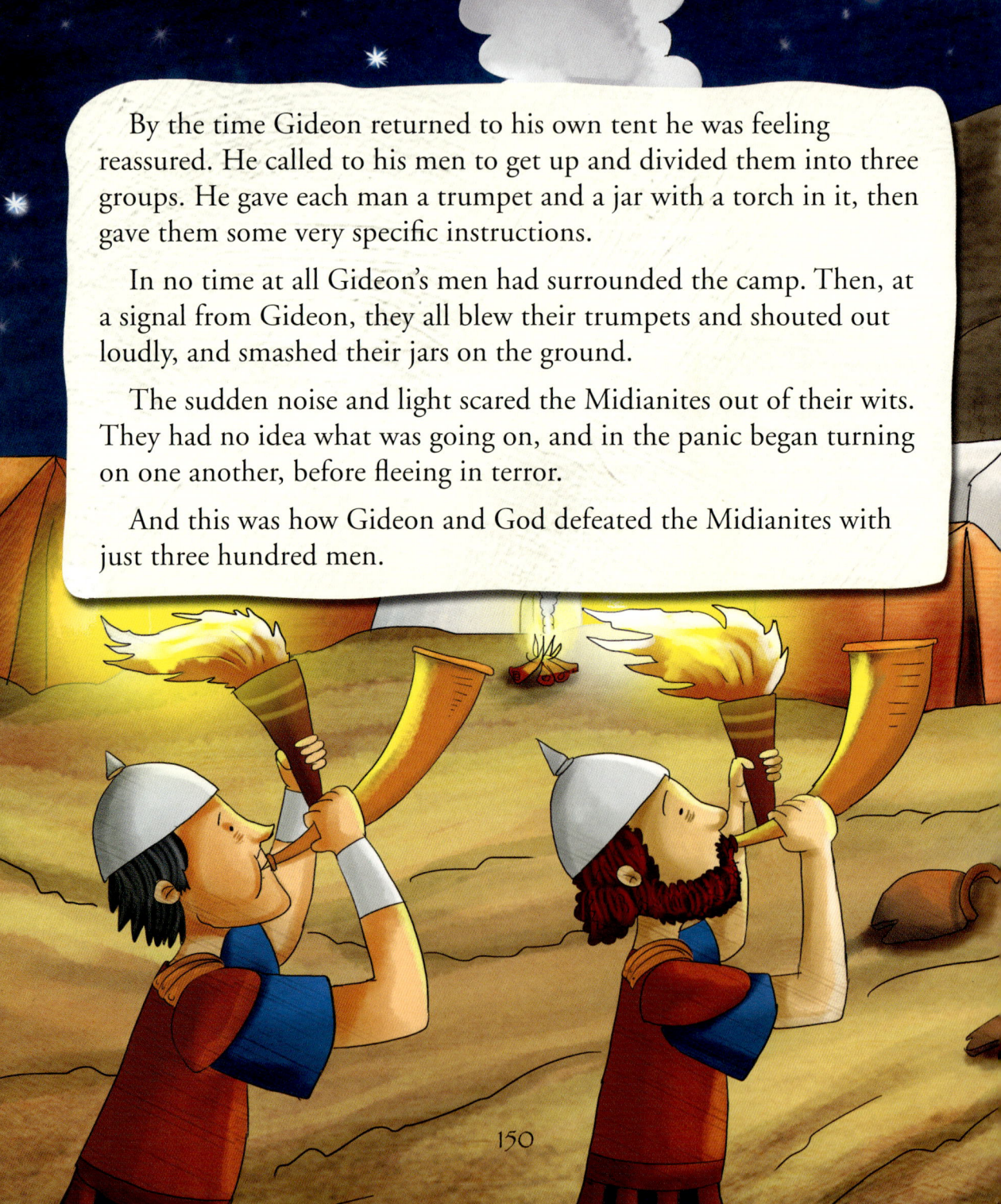

By the time Gideon returned to his own tent he was feeling reassured. He called to his men to get up and divided them into three groups. He gave each man a trumpet and a jar with a torch in it, then gave them some very specific instructions.

In no time at all Gideon's men had surrounded the camp. Then, at a signal from Gideon, they all blew their trumpets and shouted out loudly, and smashed their jars on the ground.

The sudden noise and light scared the Midianites out of their wits. They had no idea what was going on, and in the panic began turning on one another, before fleeing in terror.

And this was how Gideon and God defeated the Midianites with just three hundred men.

A Loyal Daughter-in-Law

"I'm staying with you, and that's that!" Ruth said kindly but firmly.

Naomi looked at her with tears in her eyes. Ruth wasn't even her own daughter—she had been married to one of Naomi's sons, but he had died a while ago, along with his brother. Naomi had decided that it was time to head back to her home town of Bethlehem. Her husband, too, was long dead, and she was all alone in the world apart from her two daughters-in-law. She had told them to stay behind, for she knew that her life in Bethlehem would be hard. Orpah had reluctantly said good-bye and had gone home to her family. But Ruth would not leave her.

"You shouldn't come with me," begged Naomi. "I have nothing to give you. You should be like Orpah—she has gone home to her own people and her own gods. You should do the same, my dear."

"Please don't make me leave you!" cried Ruth. "Let me go with you! Wherever you go, I will go. Your people will be my people. Your God will be my God. Don't ask me to go!"

So it was that Ruth and Naomi travelled to Bethlehem. There, life was difficult, just as Naomi had warned. But Ruth was not easily disheartened.

It was harvest time, and she decided to go into the fields where the people were working. "Maybe they will let me gather some of the grain that they drop," she said to Naomi hopefully.

The field belonged to a rich man named Boaz. When he saw Ruth in the fields he told his workers to share their food with her and to be kind to her. And he told her not to bother to go to any other fields, she would always be welcome in his. For Boaz had heard about the loyal young girl who had accompanied Naomi on her return. "God will reward you for your loyalty to Naomi," he said.

And Ruth was touched by his kindness.

Now, it turned out that Boaz was related to Naomi. When Ruth returned home with a basket full of grain and told her mother-in-law what had happened, Naomi knew that God was looking after them. And look after them he did, for in time Boaz married Ruth, and they had a beautiful baby boy, and Naomi became a proud and devoted grandmother.

Do you know what the name Naomi means? It means happy. And for the first time in a long, long while, that was exactly what Naomi was!

Samson the Strong

There was once a man named Samson who was strong. And I mean really, *really* strong! He was so strong that he had once overpowered a wild lion with his bare hands! When he was born, his parents had promised God that they would never cut his hair. It showed that he belonged to God in a very special way.

At that time the Hebrews were tormented by their enemies, the Philistines. Samson did everything that he could to be a thorn in the side of these Philistines. He carried out many raids and attacks, and the Philistines grew well and truly frustrated with him. How could he be so strong? They were desperate to know where his unbelievable strength came from. And when Samson fell in love, they seized their chance.

Delilah, the woman that Samson fell in love with, was very beautiful, but she wasn't very loyal. The Philistines offered her copious quantities of silver if she would find out the secret of Samson's strength so that they could use it against him and find a way to control him. And Delilah was happy to oblige.

Samson, however, didn't prove very keen to divulge his secret. To be sure, when Delilah first asked him he told her some half-baked story about not being able to resist if he were tied up in fresh bowstrings. Delilah promptly asked the Philistines for some fresh bowstrings, tied up Samson with them (presumably he was either fast asleep or simply humouring her!) and then watched as he broke free from them with no more effort than a leaf falling from a tree.

"You lied to me," she pouted. "You made me look stupid!" and she sulked until Samson told her that if someone tied him up with new ropes then he would be as weak as a newborn babe.

Having learned nothing from the first incident, Delilah rushed to fetch new rope, used it to bind him up tightly … then watched as he broke the ropes as easily as if they were threads of cotton.

"Hmmmph! You tricked me again!" said treacherous Delilah. "How could you do this to me!"

And so Samson spun her another yarn about weaving the braids of hair on his head with a loom. Once again she fell into the trap, and once again her plan failed.

Now Delilah was really irritated. "How can you say you love me when you obviously don't trust me?" she whined. "All you want to do is make me look foolish! If you really loved me you would tell me." And she went on, and on, and on about it until Samson could stand it no longer. To shut her up once and for all he finally told her that he had been dedicated to God before he was born, and that he had never had his hair cut.

"If someone were to cut my hair," he said wearily, "then I would be as weak as any other man." And he hoped that she would finally leave him alone.

But of course, Delilah had no such intention.

When Samson next awoke it was to find his hair shaved and his strength well and truly gone. The Philistines took him away, tore out his eyes, and placed him in chains. But soon his hair started to grow back …

Some time later the Philistine rulers held a huge celebration in their temple, attended by thousands of people. They told the guards to bring out Samson so that they could make fun of their once invincible enemy, now in chains. Samson was placed between two mighty columns which held up the temple.

While the Philistines laughed and mocked and drank and ate, Samson prayed to God to give him strength one final time. And then he took hold of the two columns, one to his left and one to his right, and he pushed them with all his might. The columns groaned and creaked, and cracks began to appear, and then, with an almighty thunder, the columns fell and the temple collapsed on Samson and the rulers and everyone else that was there!

And so, in his final act, Samson killed more Philistines than he had done in the rest of his lifetime.

A Voice in the Night

Young Samuel was fast slept in the temple. As soon as he had been old enough, his mother had brought him to the temple, for he had been promised to God. Now Eli, the priest, looked after him, and Samuel loved God with all his heart.

All of a sudden Samuel awoke with a start. He had heard someone calling his name. He rushed through to Eli to see what he needed, but Eli said, "I didn't call you, child. Go back to bed!"

Puzzled but sleepy, Samuel made his way back to bed. He had hardly laid his head down when again he heard his name clearly called, "Samuel!"

Once again, he went through to Eli … and Eli sent him straight back to bed, protesting that he hadn't called him.

When this happened a third time, Eli realised what was going on. It was God! God was calling Samuel! He said to the young boy, "Go back to bed, and the next time that God speaks to you answer him, 'I am here, Lord. I am your servant and I am listening.'"

So that was just what Samuel did, and God warned him that some unpleasant things were going to happen soon in Israel.

This was the first time that God spoke to Samuel, but it was not the last, for Samuel came to be one of the greatest of prophets that Israel ever saw, and carried out the Lord's work for the rest of his life.

The Shepherd Boy

The people of Israel had demanded a king. No matter that God looked out for them. No matter that Samuel was at the helm. No matter that your average king would exploit the people, cream off their wealth, and start unnecessary wars (that the people would have to fight)! Nope, they wanted a king and they wouldn't shut up until they had one.

The first one (Saul) started off well, but ended up on the wrong track. So God chose a new king and sent Samuel to anoint him. Samuel found himself at the house of Jesse in Bethlehem. Now Jesse had eight sons and God had told him that one of these would be the future king of Israel.

When Samuel arrived, Jesse brought his eldest son before the prophet.

Eliab was tall and handsome. Samuel thought it must surely be him—he fit the role perfectly!

"You are looking at the outside, not the inside," cautioned God. "Don't judge by appearances. This is not the right man."

So Jesse brought forward his second son, and then his third, and fourth and so on.

They were all fine, strong-looking young men, and Samuel was sure each time that this must be the one whom God had in mind. But each time God told him that this was not the one.

Samuel had seen seven of Jesse's sons. "Do you have any more sons?" he asked, feeling rather puzzled.

"Just the one—David. He is out in the fields with the sheep. He is my youngest son."

When David was brought to Samuel, God said straight away, "This is the one. Anoint him!"

It would be a while before David would take the throne, but from that day onwards the spirit of the Lord was with David always.

A Stone in a Sling

The Israelites were at war with the Philistines—again!—and the two great armies had come together to do battle. David had brought food to his brothers who were in the army, and when he arrived he found the camp in turmoil.

For forty days they had been subjected to taunts and ridicule from their enemy. Specifically, from one particular soldier—a man named Goliath. Now, calling him a man doesn't really do him justice. You see, Goliath was over nine feet tall. He was practically a giant! He wore heavy bronze armour, and a bronze helmet and had a bronze javelin strapped to his back. He was fierce and strong and absolutely terrifying. And every morning for the last forty days he had come forward and challenged the Israelites to a duel. "I dare you to find one man in your so-called army brave enough to fight me!" he roared. "If he wins and kills me then we will be your slaves. But if I win, then you will all serve us!"

The Israelite soldiers were quaking in their boots. Not one of them dared to face this mighty giant.

But when David heard about what was happening, he put down his bag of food and said calmly, "Let me go. I will fight him."

Some of the soldiers took David to the king, Saul. David said to the king, "I will fight this Philistine. He has no right to make fun of the army of God!"

Saul looked at the boy in disbelief. "Are you out of your mind? You're a boy—not a soldier! And what makes you think that you can fight this Goliath when all of my men are terrified of him?"

"I might only be a shepherd boy," replied David quietly, "but I am used to fighting off the wild animals that come for my sheep. I have killed both a lion and a bear. I am not scared. God will be with me."

Saul hardly knew what to say. This self-possessed young boy puzzled him—and if truth be told, rather impressed him.

He agreed that David could take on the challenge, and offered him his own royal armour and his own sword. But David did not feel comfortable in them. It was not what he was used to.

Instead, he took his walking staff and went down to a stream where he chose five smooth stones. He put these in his bag, and held his sling in his hand. And then he went to face the Philistine.

Goliath laughed when he saw him coming. This was his opponent? This child? This shepherd boy? He didn't even have a sword. The Israelites must have lost their minds!

"Don't think I'll go easy on you," he jeered. "When I've finished with you (which won't take a minute) I'll feed your body to the birds and wild animals!"

David stood before him bravely. "You have your armour and your spear and your sword. But I have God! You shouldn't have said all those bad things about him. Today God will let me defeat you. And it is *I* who will feed *your* body to the birds and animals. Along with the rest of your army!"

Goliath was furious. How dare this little upstart talk to him like that? He moved forward with his sword ready, but David was faster.

Approaching the warrior at a run, David deftly put one of the smooth stones in his sling, swung it expertly around his head, and fired it straight at Goliath. And his aim was unerring. It hit the giant right in the middle of his forehead—right between the eyes.

And Goliath fell to the ground, face first!

Then David took Goliath's own sword, and used it to cut off his enemy's head!

When the other Philistines saw the fall of their champion they were filled with fear and fled the battlefield on the spot. David had saved the day.

And that is how a young shepherd boy defeated Goliath with just a stone and a sling (and God's help, of course!)

It doesn't matter how small and unimportant we might feel, nor does it matter how those around us see us. God has a role for all of us! He can use each and every one of us to carry out his work!

The Secret Signal

David was a hero, but it wasn't quite yet time for him to be king, for Saul still sat on the throne.

At first Saul was pleased with David. He even brought him to live in the royal palace, where David became very close to Saul's son, Jonathan. But soon Saul grew jealous. David became a renowned soldier, and seemed to win battles wherever the king sent him, and the people loved him. They began to cheer louder for David than they did for Saul, and that didn't please the king one little bit!

One day when David was playing the harp Saul suddenly flipped and threw a spear at him for the king was filled with an evil spirit! David leapt out of the way, but Saul tried again! Again, the spear missed. Now Saul felt afraid. His aim was usually pretty good—so it was all too clear that God wasn't interested in him any more and was looking after David!

Time and again Saul tried to have David killed. In the end David had to flee the palace. Jonathan desperately hoped that he could calm his father down, and make him stop, so that David could come back. He promised his friend that he would talk to his father, and then they arranged a special secret signal so that David would know whether or not it was safe to come home.

"I will shoot three arrows," said Jonathan to David, " and then I will tell my servant to fetch them. If I say to him, "You've gone too far, the arrows are closer to me!" then it is safe for you to come back. But if I say to the servant, "The arrows are further away. Go and get them," then you must leave, for my father means to kill you."

The next day, David hid behind some bushes and watched as his friend came into the field with his servant. Jonathan fired the arrows, and how David's heart sank when he heard his friend call to his servant, "The arrows are further away. Hurry! Don't just stand there—go and fetch them!"

As the servant disappeared to look for the arrows, David emerged from the bushes and the two friends hugged sadly. They knew they might never see one another again.

The Shepherd King

David had a difficult time ahead of him, for he was now an outlaw, hunted by the king. But he never gave up trusting in God.

Some time later the Philistines marched upon Saul and his army. David was not there. Both Jonathan and Saul were killed in the battle, along with many, many soldiers. When David found out, he wept.

Now David was anointed king over Judah, but in the north of the land, another son of Saul, Ish-Bosheth, was anointed king of Israel. For some time there were two kings in Israel and it was a time of turmoil and conflict. David's side was winning, but the fighting only finally ended when Ish-Bosheth was murdered.

Now David was truly the king of Israel.

This was not the way David wanted his reign to start, but from now on, things would be better. And the very first thing he did was to head for Jerusalem, which was held by a Canaanite tribe.

Everyone thought that the city was impenetrable. The people inside it definitely thought so. In fact, when David and his soldiers marched to the city, the people inside laughed at them. "You'll never get in!" they taunted. "Don't waste your time! The blind and the lame could defend us!" You see, the city was protected by high walls and huge gates, and was surrounded by hills.

But David had other plans. He had found out that there was a water tunnel leading all the way into the heart of the city. His men climbed up it, opened the gates from the inside, and so the mighty city fell!

David had conquered Jerusalem and he made it his capital city, with the Ark of the Covenant at its very heart. He went on to be one of the greatest of all kings of Israel. He did make mistakes, but when he did he was filled with remorse. He stayed true to God all his life, and died a peaceful death.

Solomon the Wise

Solomon was the son of David. For many, many years his father had ruled over Israel and Judah. But now the throne belonged to Solomon.

Soon after he had been crowned, Solomon was visited by God in a dream.

"What would you like me to give you, Solomon?" asked God. "Name it, and it shall be yours."

Solomon did not hesitate in his reply. "I am young," he said, "and inexperienced. Please make me wise, so that I might be a good king like my father—so that I might rule over your people as they deserve. Help me to know the difference between right and wrong."

God was pleased with Solomon. "You might have asked for riches or power," he replied. "You might have asked for long life or health. But you didn't. You have asked for wisdom, and you shall have it. But you shall have all the other things that you didn't ask for too! Follow in my ways and you will live a long and prosperous life."

When Solomon awoke from his dream, he was filled with a sense of well-being. God was pleased with him. God was looking out for him.

Solomon soon became known throughout the land for his wisdom. People travelled for miles and miles to seek his judgement.

One day two women came before the king. And they were quarrelling over a child—a baby boy!

"Your Majesty," pleaded one. "This woman stole my son! We live together in the same house, and both gave birth to sons at the same time. But hers died and the next night while I was sleeping, she took my healthy son and placed her dead son in his crib in his place!"

"Lies!" cried the second woman. "It was her son who died! This is mine!"

And so they argued.

Now, this was long before such things as DNA tests. There was no way to tell which was the real mother. How could Solomon be expected to sort this mess out?

"You both insist that the living son is yours, and that the dead child belongs to the other woman," said Solomon, and the women nodded.

Then he called to one of his servants to fetch a sword. "Cut the baby in two," he ordered the servant. "Then each woman may have half of it."

The second woman said, "Yes, that is fair. Then neither of us will have him!"

But the real mother, the first woman, gasped out in horror, "No! Stop! Don't harm my baby. Give him to the other woman—yes, do!—but don't hurt him! Please! I beg you!"

Then Solomon told the servant to give the child to the first woman. "It is her child," he said. "She is the real mother, for she would do anything to keep her baby safe."

When news of this got around everyone saw how wise and clever God had made Solomon.

The Special Temple

God chose Solomon for a very special task. He had him build a temple in the heart of Jerusalem.

The temple would be a holy building, a house of God, and a home for the Ark of the Covenant. All the stones—great big stones—were quarried and hewn well away from the building site, so that the stones could be laid quietly and reverently.

It took seven years, and thousands of men, to build the temple. The Ark was carefully placed in the Inner Temple, which had walls of beautiful cedar, carved with images, and big, heavy doors, covered with the finest gold. There the Ark rested under the gaze of two cherubim, each made of olive wood and covered in gold, and fifteen feet high!

When it was finished, the temple was filled with God's presence, and the people praised him, full of gratitude and awe.

"I know that you, Lord, who created heaven and earth, would never live in a building made by men," said Solomon. "But I pray that in this building we can be close to you and hear your word."

And God told Solomon that he had heard his prayer and that his heart and eyes would be in the temple, and that for as long as the king loved and obeyed God, he would always be with him.

Elijah and the Ravens

Elijah was another of God's prophets. Israel had split in two—after the death of King Solomon the tribes of Judah and Benjamin stayed loyal to Solomon's son, but the ten northern tribes broke away. Now wicked King Ahab was the ruler of the northern kingdom and he allowed the worship of the false god, Baal. Elijah had his work cut out to try to bring the people back to God.

God sent a drought throughout the land. Elijah warned the king that for the next few years there would be neither rain nor dew throughout the land. Needless to say, Ahab wasn't too thrilled with this news. And he wasn't pleased with Elijah.

God sent Elijah away to a safe place, where ravens brought him food every morning and every evening, and he drank from a small brook.

Elijah and the Widow

At last even the faithful brook dried up. Now God sent Elijah to a place named Sidon, where he promised that a widow would help him.

Sure enough, when Elijah came to the city gates he spotted a poor widow collecting a few straggly sticks. He went up to her and asked, "Please will you bring me a little water?"

Now, with the drought, there was very little water to be had, but the kind widow turned straight away to go and fetch some for the thirsty prophet. As she was going, Elijah called out, "And would you mind bringing me just a tiny bit of bread?"

The woman turned and smiled sadly. "I am afraid I have no bread. At home all I have is a handful of flour and a little oil in a jar. I was gathering a few sticks so that I could take them home. Then I was going to use up the last of the flour and oil to make some bread for my son and me to eat before we die."

Elijah said soothingly, "Don't worry. Carry on doing what you were going to do, but first make a small loaf of bread and bring it to me, and then make some for you and your son. For God has promised that the flour and the oil will not run out before the drought ends!"

The trusting widow did as the prophet had asked, and she was amazed to find that when she had made the loaves of bread there was still flour and oil left over. And so it went on, for every day when she made bread there was still enough flour and oil to make another loaf!

But although the widow and her son did not go hungry, the little boy fell ill—desperately ill. And all too soon he stopped breathing!

The widow was distraught. "Why did you ever come here?" she said to Elijah despairingly. "Did you come to punish me by killing my son?"

Elijah replied calmly, "Give me your son," and he carried the boy to the room upstairs that he was using, and placed him gently on his bed. Then he cried out to God, "Oh Lord, why have you brought such a tragedy upon this woman? She has been so good to me!"

He stretched out upon the boy three times, and called to God again, and begged him to bring him back to life.

God heard Elijah's prayer, and the boy once again began to breathe. Elijah carried him downstairs to his mother, who wept tears of joy when she saw that her beloved son was alive.

"You truly are a man of God!" she said, filled with happiness and gratitude.

Battle of the Prophets

After three years Elijah told King Ahab to gather the people of Israel and the prophets of Baal at Mount Carmel.

"It is time for you to learn who is the true God of Israel!" he said, and he proposed a contest. Both he and the prophets of Baal should prepare a bull for sacrifice (there were four hundred and fifty of them, and just one of him, but whatever). But they were not to start the fire themselves. They were to leave that up to their god. No matches or burning torches in play—only the power of prayer!

Well, the prophets of Baal were happy to go first. After all, there were rather a few of them. It should be a doddle.

So, they prepared their sacrifice, put it on the altar, and then they prayed. And they prayed. And they prayed.

"What's taking you?" yawned Elijah. "Is this going to take all day?"

The prophets of Baal started to tear their clothes. They got down on their hands and knees. They raised their hands to heaven. They cut themselves with swords.

Still nothing happened.

"Maybe Baal's sleeping," mocked Elijah. "Maybe you should pray a little louder! Maybe he's busy doing something else."

The prophets of Baal danced wildly around the altar. They threw themselves to the ground. They were still praying when evening came, when they fell to the ground in exhaustion.

"Enough," said Elijah. "Now it's my turn."

The altar to God had been torn down, so first of all Elijah repaired it, using twelve stones—one for each of the tribes. When it was ready, he put his meat on the altar, and then he did something very strange. He told the people to pour water all over it—over the meat, and the wood. Soon it was drenched. Then Elijah told them to pour more water over it. And then one last time. By now the water was running down the altar, and even filled a ditch that he had dug around the bottom.

The people muttered amongst themselves. What on earth was Elijah playing at?

Then God's prophet stepped forward and prayed: "Lord, let everyone know today that you are God in Israel and that I have done these things at your command."

And at that very moment fire came down from God and burned up the sacrifice, the wood, the stones, and even the water in the ditch!

The people fell to their knees. "It's true!" they cried. "The Lord is God!"

The Chariot of Fire

Elijah did many amazing things in his lifetime, but at last the time had come for him to finish his time on earth. One day he was walking by the river Jordan with his special pupil Elisha.

Elisha was sad, for he knew that Elijah would be leaving him. When Elijah asked if there was anything he wanted to request before he left, Elisha replied gravely, "Master, I should like to inherit your spirit—double your spirit!—so that I can continue your work when you are gone."

"This is not a little thing that you ask," said Elijah, "but if you see me leave you, then it will be as you wish."

And right then a chariot of fire descended from heaven, and it was drawn by horses of fire! It came between the two men, and Elijah was taken up to heaven in a whirlwind.

When the skies had calmed, Elisha saw before him Elijah's cloak, which had fallen to the ground. With a heart full of wonder and awe, of both sadness and joy, he took the cloak and walked to the bank of the river. He hit the river with the cloak and the waters parted before him and he crossed over.

As soon as the other prophets saw him they understood that Elijah's spirit had passed to Elisha, and they bowed before him in respect.

The Amazing Jar of Oil

One day a woman came to see Elisha to beg for his help. "Sir," she said desperately, "my husband has died, and he has left debts which I cannot repay. The man we owe has threatened to take my two sons as slaves in repayment. Please help!"

Now, Elisha had no money to give her—he lived a very simple life and had no use for money. But he thought carefully, and then he asked her, "What do you have at home?"

"Nothing but a jar of olive oil!" said the woman despondently.

Then Elisha gave her some very peculiar instructions. He told her to go to all her neighbours and ask them if she could borrow any empty jars that they might have. "Find as many as you possibly can!" he urged, "then go home and shut all the doors. Just you and your sons! Then pour the oil into the jars and keep them safe."

The woman was puzzled, but she did exactly as she was told. When she and her sons were in the house they closed the doors and the shutters on the windows, and gathered all the jars together. Then she began to pour the oil into one of the jars. As soon as it was full, one of her sons placed another jar in front of her, and she filled that one too, and then another, and another. She poured and poured until there were no empty jars left. And when she looked in the original jar she saw that it was empty too!

The widow and her sons were able to sell the jars of olive oil and repay their debt, and there was even money left over for them to live on!

Washed Clean

Naaman was a commander of the army of Syria. He was a renowned soldier and God had brought him many great victories, but he was feeling decidedly miserable. You see, Naaman had a terrible skin disease, and it is difficult to feel happy when you have sores all over you, itching and weeping and bothering you night and day.

It came to pass that a young Israelite girl became a slave in Naaman's household. When she saw the suffering of her master, she suggested that he should travel to see the wonderful prophet Elisha, who lived in Samaria in Israel.

Naaman asked his king if he might travel to Israel, and the king said "yes". He even wrote a letter for Naaman to give the king of Israel.

"This is my servant, Naaman," the letter said. "Cure his leprosy."

The king of Israel was rather taken aback when he read the letter. And when Naaman presented him with chests of silver and gold and fine clothes.

"I'm ever so sorry that you have this horrid skin disease," he said, scratching his head (Naaman's sores made him feel itchy himself!) "But I'm not quite sure what you expect me to do about it!"

And to himself he wondered if it was all a trick, and worried that Naaman's king was trying to start a fight!

Fortunately Elisha himself saved the day. He sent a messenger to the king telling him to send Naaman to him.

Now, when Naaman, with his servants and horses and chariot arrived at Elisha's house, he was rather disgruntled when the prophet sent his servant out to him. He probably expected the prophet to come out himself and bow down before him—and lay out a red carpet while he was at it!

But no, the servant came out with a simple message. "Go and wash in the Jordan River. Bathe in it seven times and your skin will be healed, and you will be clean."

Naaman was furious. Furious and offended! "Can Elisha not be bothered to come and heal me himself?" he sulked. "If he thinks I'm going to go and bathe in that filthy river just because he says so then he can think again. We've plenty of rivers in Syria. And they're far less stinky!"

He was on the point of storming off in disgust when his servant managed to persuade him that he might as well give it a try.

So Naaman swallowed his pride and went down to the river and dipped himself in it seven times. And guess what? When he emerged after the seventh time all the sores had completely disappeared and his skin was soft and smooth and healthy.

He rushed to thank Elisha. He stood before the prophet and bowed his head. "Now I know that yours is the one true God!"

The Power of Prayer

The years passed. Israel fell into disgrace. Its kings and its people turned from God and fell into wicked ways. When the armies of Assyria turned upon Israel, God did not help him. He knew that it was time to punish his children. He had given them so many chances, but now they had to learn their lesson the hard way. Samaria fell, and the Israelites were forced to leave their country.

In the south, Hezekiah was king, and he refused to make an alliance with Assyria. Hezekiah was a good man, who placed his trust in God. And he also had the wise prophet Isaiah by his side. So when the mighty Assyrian army came knocking at the gates of Jerusalem, Hezekiah refused to panic.

"Don't be afraid," Isaiah told the people of Jerusalem as they cowered in fear. "Don't make the same mistake as Israel. Trust in God. He will save us."

The commander of the Assyrians sent a message: "Your God won't save you! Look at what happened to Samaria! Your only option is to give up. If you surrender now, then I will be merciful!"

Hezekiah went to the temple where he prayed. "Lord, don't let these people insult you like this. Save us, so that everyone can see just how powerful you are—so that everyone can see that you are the one true God!"

When Hezekiah and Isaiah and the people of Jerusalem awoke the next morning, it was to a strange hush outside the city walls. For during the night an angel of the Lord had passed over the enemy camp and the sun had risen on the dead bodies of thousands of Assyrian soldiers. And those that were spared fled for their lives as quickly as they could!

There is no army big enough to overcome God!

The Potter and His Clay

Hezekiah had been a good king, but not all those who ruled after him obeyed God as they should. The years passed and Judah and Jerusalem turned further and further away from God.

God sent another prophet to warn them. Jeremiah had a hard task. People didn't want to listen to his message. They didn't like being told that what they were doing was wrong. They just wanted him to shut up and leave them in peace. But Jeremiah knew he couldn't do that.

One day he sat in a potter's workshop, watching him at work. The potter took pieces of rough clay, then skillfully and lovingly shaped them into beautiful vases and useful plates and bowls. But sometimes the clay didn't do what the potter wanted it to do. Then he would start again and make it into something different.

"Israel is like the clay," God told Jeremiah. "I am trying to mould something special out of it, something wonderful. But if it doesn't work out then I am prepared to start again from scratch. If Israel becomes evil, then I will change what I had planned for it, but if it repents then I will give it another chance."

Jeremiah tried to warn the people. But they wouldn't listen. Instead they threw him in jail!

Conquered!

The people had refused to listen to God's warnings. They had been given their final chance. Their time was nearly up.

Jerusalem fell to a new enemy—Babylon, and its mighty ruler, Nebuchadnezzar. All the strong, skilled people from the city were taken away to Babylon to work. Those who were left behind thanked their lucky stars. But actually they were in a worse position. Those who had been sent to Babylon had had time to repent and were beginning to look to God again. But those left in Jerusalem were stuck in their ways.

The new king—who had been placed there by Nebuchadnezzar—began to think that he was powerful enough to stand up to Babylon. Jeremiah tried to warn him, but the king would not listen. And as night follows day, Babylon once again bore down on the city of Jerusalem and this time they burned the city to the ground.

God had punished his children, but he had not stopped loving them. He knew that they had needed this hard lesson, and that they would learn from it. They would return to his open arms, and one day they would come home, with God by their side.

But for now, they were exiled from their beloved land.

The Valley of Bones

Ezekiel was one of those exiles. He had warned his fellow exiles that Jerusalem would fall, and fall it did. When the exiles learnt of the destruction of their beloved city and the holy temple they wept. "God has abandoned us for good!" they wailed, hopelessly. They were filled with despair.

But God didn't want them to give up and wallow in self-pity. They had been disobedient, they had turned their back on him—but he wanted them to learn from their mistakes. He wanted them to understand where they had gone wrong, and he wanted them to want to make it right. When they had truly learnt their lesson, then he would forgive them, and they could start over.

God wanted Ezekiel to pass his message on to the people. He showed him something so that he could understand.

He took Ezekiel to a dry valley. As far as Ezekiel could see the dusty, stony ground was covered in bones—human bones! The prophet wandered across the floor of the valley, stepping between the bones. They were dry, and scoured by the wind and dust. Ezekiel shivered.

"Do you think these bones can live, Ezekiel?" God asked him.

Ezekiel didn't quite know what to say. "Only you know that, my Lord," he replied.

"Speak to the bones for me, Ezekiel," God continued. "Tell them that they will come to life. Tell them that I will put sinew and muscles on them, and cover them with skin. And that I will breath life into them and they will live again."

Ezekiel knew better than to doubt God. He did exactly as he had been told. He said the words that God had told him to say.

And while he was still speaking he began to hear a noise—a rattling and scraping and scratching—all across the valley, and the bones began to come together and make skeletons. And while he looked, muscles and sinews bound the bones together, and then skin covered

the bodies. And then—and this was the most amazing thing of all—a wind blew across the valley and breathed life into the still bodies, and one by one they rose to their feet and stood there in the valley, silently waiting, a vast army of men.

"My people are like these bones," said God, as Ezekiel looked upon the amazing sight. "It is as if they were dead. They have lost hope. They are lifeless and ruined. But that is not the end. I will breathe life into them once again. They will rise anew, and I will lead them back to Israel. Go and speak to them, Ezekiel. Go and tell them that I will do this."

God wanted Ezekiel to give hope to his people. Now the prophet must go and tell them that God would breathe new life into them!

The Daniel Diet

Daniel was another of the exiles in Babylon. He came from a good family and was clever and strong and handsome. And that was why he, and three of his friends, were specially chosen to be trained to serve King Nebuchadnezzar himself.

The young men were taken to the palace where they were taught the language and history of the land. They were treated well and the king ordered that they should eat the very same food and drink the very same wine that he did.

From the sounds of it, this was a pretty good deal. The king had the best of everything! There was just one problem. God had told the Israelites what food to eat to keep them healthy (having made humans in the first place, God probably had a pretty good idea about what foods would be good for them and what wouldn't.) And Daniel always listened to God. So he did not want to eat the rich food that the royal court enjoyed, or drink wine every day with his meals as they did.

He spoke to the official whose job it was to oversee the trainees—a man named Ashpenaz. He told him that he and his friends just wanted to eat vegetables and drink water—as God had commanded.

Ashpenaz was rather flummoxed. "I'd really like to help," he said, "but if I feed you just vegetables and water you will get ill and become weak. Have you any idea what the king will do to me if anything happens to you! He'd kill me!" (and he was probably right—Nebuchadnezzar was not known for his patience or compassion!)

Daniel didn't give up. He spoke to the guard who brought their food. "Just try it for ten days," he urged. "Give us vegetables and water for ten days, and see what happens."

The guard agreed, and after ten days it was clear to see that Daniel and his friends were fitter and healthier than all the other young men who had been eating the king's rich food. And so they were allowed to continue.

The Mysterious Dream

The training period had finished and Daniel and his friends had come out the other end with flying colours. These four were chosen to be special advisors to the king himself, and the king found them more use than any of the magicians or wise men in his kingdom.

But one night Nebuchadnezzar had a very disturbing dream. He was so troubled by it that he called all his advisors to him to help—all his magicians and sorcerers and wise men.

"Tell me what my dream means!" he demanded.

The advisors waited. They thought something else was coming. They thought he was going to tell them exactly what his dream had been about.

But they thought wrong!

"Err, Your Majesty," said one of them hesitantly, "aren't you going to tell us what the dream was?"

"Just work it out yourselves," said the king rather unreasonably. "That's what I'm paying you for!"

When the advisors shuffled and mumbled and muttered something about only the gods being able to do such a thing, the king completely lost his cool. He ordered the execution of every last one of them!

Now, this order included Daniel and his friends (even though they hadn't been there at the time). Daniel begged Nebuchadnezzar for a little more time—which he was granted—and then he and his friends spent all night praying to God to help them.

The next day Daniel went to the king. "Your Majesty," he said, "this is what you saw in your dream—

"You saw a huge and terrible statue standing in front of you. Its head was made of shining gold, its chest and arms were made of silver, its waist and hips of bronze, its legs of iron and its feet were a mixture of iron and clay.

"As you watched a massive stone fell into it. It smashed the feet into pieces, and then the whole statue crumbled and fell away into dust and was blown away on the breeze. But the stone grew into a mountain that covered the whole earth."

Nebuchadnezzar said nothing. Probably a good sign.

Daniel continued. "Your dream foretells the future. It foretells what will happen after your reign. The head is like the mighty empire of Babylon. The other parts of the statue are empires yet to come, each replacing the one before it.

"But the stone—the stone will be a new kingdom that God will set up. This kingdom will destroy all those that have gone before it, and it will last forever! This stone will become a mountain!"

Nebuchadnezzar had to admit he was impressed. With Daniel, and with Daniel's God. "Your God truly is the God of gods!" he cried, and he made Daniel his chief advisor.

The Fiery Furnace

Unfortunately, Nebuchadnezzar soon forgot about how impressed he was with God. He made some very dubious decisions.

One time he decided to have an enormous statue built out of gold—ninety feet high, and nine feet wide! He gathered everyone together in a special ceremony. The herald announced, "Hear me, people of the Empire! When you hear the sound of the horn, the pipe, the drum and all the other musical instruments, you are to bow down and worship the statue that King Nebuchadnezzar has put up. Anyone who fails to do so will be thrown into a blazing furnace!"

And so, as soon as they heard the sound of the horn, the pipe, the drum and all the other musical instruments everyone bowed down before the statue and worshipped it. Well, not quite everyone. In the crowd were Daniel's three friends, Shadrach, Meshach, and Abednego (these were their Babylonian names). Like Daniel, these men worshipped God alone. There was no way that they were going to bow down before a golden idol. No way at all!

Now, if you think that the king might go easy on his favourite advisors, then think again. He ordered the guards to bring the men before him. "How dare you disobey my command? I'll give you one last chance to bow down before the idol. If not, I will have you thrown into the furnace, and nothing and nobody will be able to save you then!"

"Our God can save us from the furnace if he chooses to," replied the men calmly. "But even if he doesn't, we shall not bow down before your idol. It doesn't matter what you do to us!"

Nebuchadnezzar was furious. Hopping mad! So mad in fact, that he told the guards to heat the furnace up seven times hotter than normal. Then they tied up the friends as tight as they could and threw them in—oh, and by the way, the furnace was so hot that the guards who threw the men in were scorched to death!

Nebuchadnezzar looked on (from a safe distance, of course!) After a moment, he scratched his head and turned to the official by his side. "Didn't the guards tie them up properly?" the king demanded.

"I'm certain they did, Your Majesty," the official stuttered.

"And I thought there were only three of them?"

"There were, Your Majesty!" gulped the official.

"Then how come I can see four men walking around in there without a care in the world—and one of them looks like the Son of God?!"

Not surprisingly the official didn't have an answer for that!

King Nebuchadnezzar stepped forward and called out to the men to come out of the fire. Everyone could see that their clothes were untouched—no burns or scorch marks—and their skin wasn't even red. I mean, honestly! They didn't even smell of smoke!

"Praise the God of Shadrach, Meshach, and Abednego!" said Nebuchadnezzar. "You were willing to give up your lives to follow his commands and he came and saved you from the fire. Your God can do wonderful things! There is no other god like him!"

And the king decreed that no one in his land should speak out against God. If they did, they would be punished (and we have already established that Nebuchadnezzar was pretty good at coming up with punishments!)

Daniel and the Lions

While it looked as if Nebuchadnezzar had learnt a valuable lesson, I'm sorry to say he soon forgot it again. To be honest, he was far more interested in himself than in any god. And the same can be said for most of the kings who came after him.

Some time had passed and Daniel was still an advisor to the king, but now it was Darius the Mede who sat on the throne. Darius had taken quite a shine to Daniel. He quickly realised that the Israelite was clever and honest and trustworthy, and he decided to make Daniel his second in command.

This might have gone better had not the king's other advisors been consumed with jealousy. "Why should a stupid foreigner have so much power?" they muttered to one another. "Why should the king favour him above us? We have to do something about him!"

Now, Daniel never did anything wrong so it was going to be difficult to get him into trouble. But they thought, and they watched, and they plotted, and in the end they came up with a sneaky plan to get rid of him.

"Your Majesty," said the advisors to Darius, "we all think that you should make a law that for thirty days no one should ask for anything from any god or man except you, O Mighty Ruler! And if they do, then they should be thrown into the lions' den!"

Maybe Darius wasn't listening properly, or maybe he felt bullied into it, or maybe he just liked the idea of being so powerful. Whatever the case, he agreed to the new decree, and signed it personally—at which point it became set in stone, and couldn't be changed or retracted, according to the law of the land.

What the underhand advisors had realised was that every day Daniel went to his window to pray—in the morning, at noon, and again at night. Every day, without fail. Daniel loved to talk to God.

Daniel heard about the king's decree, but the next morning he went to his window and prayed, just like always.

The other officials rubbed their hands in glee when they saw him there, and marched straight to the king.

"Your Majesty," they said pompously, "it has sadly come to our attention that someone is disobeying your new law!"

"Oh?" said the king. "And who is that?"

"I'm afraid it is Daniel, Your Majesty. He is still praying to his God not once, not twice, but three times a day! He has no respect for your law!"

The king was crestfallen. But what could he do? He thought and thought, but the law could not be cancelled. It couldn't even be changed. In the end he had no choice. To the lions' pit Daniel must go!

As Darius watched the rock being moved to cover the entrance, he called down to Daniel sadly, "I hope that your God can save you!" And then Daniel was left to the lions.

Darius went miserably back to the palace. They tried to send jesters and musicians to cheer him up, but he sent them away. They prepared a fine meal for him, but he sent that away too. He finally went to bed, but he spent a sleepless night, tossing and turning, and cursing his officials and advisors for the mess they had put him in.

The next morning at the crack of dawn the king went straight down to the pit and ordered the guards to lift up the stone.

"Daniel," he called. "Are you there? Has your God been able to save you?"

Imagine his surprise when Daniel called back, "My King, may you live forever! God sent his angel to save me. He closed the lions' mouths. God knew I had done nothing wrong, so the lions have not hurt me!"

Darius called to the guards to bring Daniel out immediately. He inspected every inch of his body—he could hardly believe his eyes! He couldn't find even the smallest, tiniest scratch! Daniel was unharmed!

The king wrote a new law for all the people throughout his kingdom, telling them to fear and respect Daniel's God, for he was the one true God, and could perform miracles!

Then Darius called for all those advisors and officials who had accused Daniel in the first place to be brought to the lions' den. And without an ounce of remorse he ordered the guards to throw them to the lions. And this time the lions had a veritable feast!

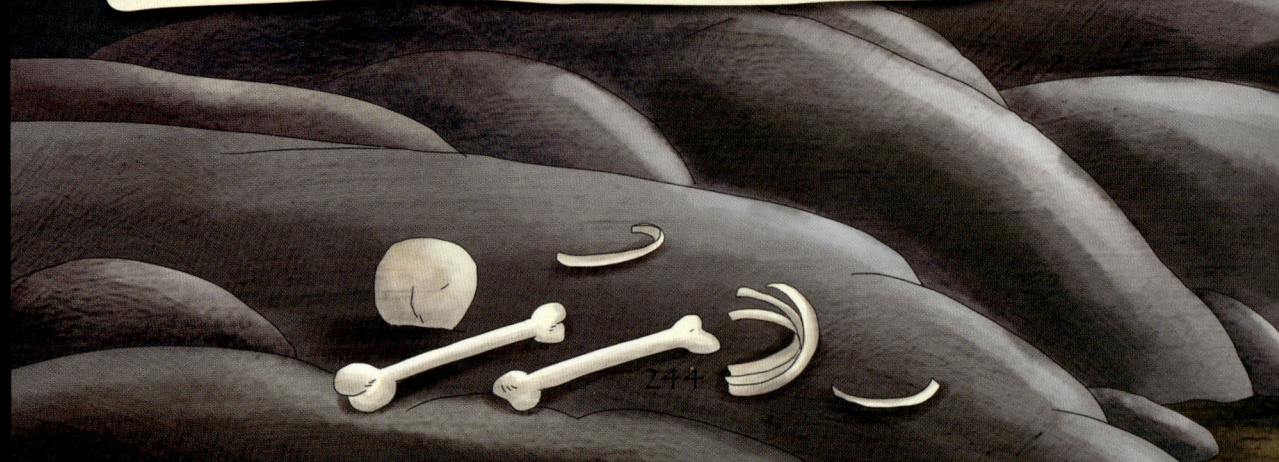

Rebuilding Jerusalem

When Daniel was an old man, the new ruler of the empire finally allowed the exiles to return home to Jerusalem.

While filled with joy at their homecoming, they had an uphill battle ahead of them. Not only was their city devastated, the walls ruined, and the holy temple looted and wrecked, but there were new people living in their land—people who were not thrilled at the return of the Jews and who didn't want them to rebuild their city. These new neighbours were the Samaritans, and they made life as difficult as they could for the returning Jews. But God sent prophets to encourage and guide the people, and at last the temple was rebuilt.

But still the people struggled.

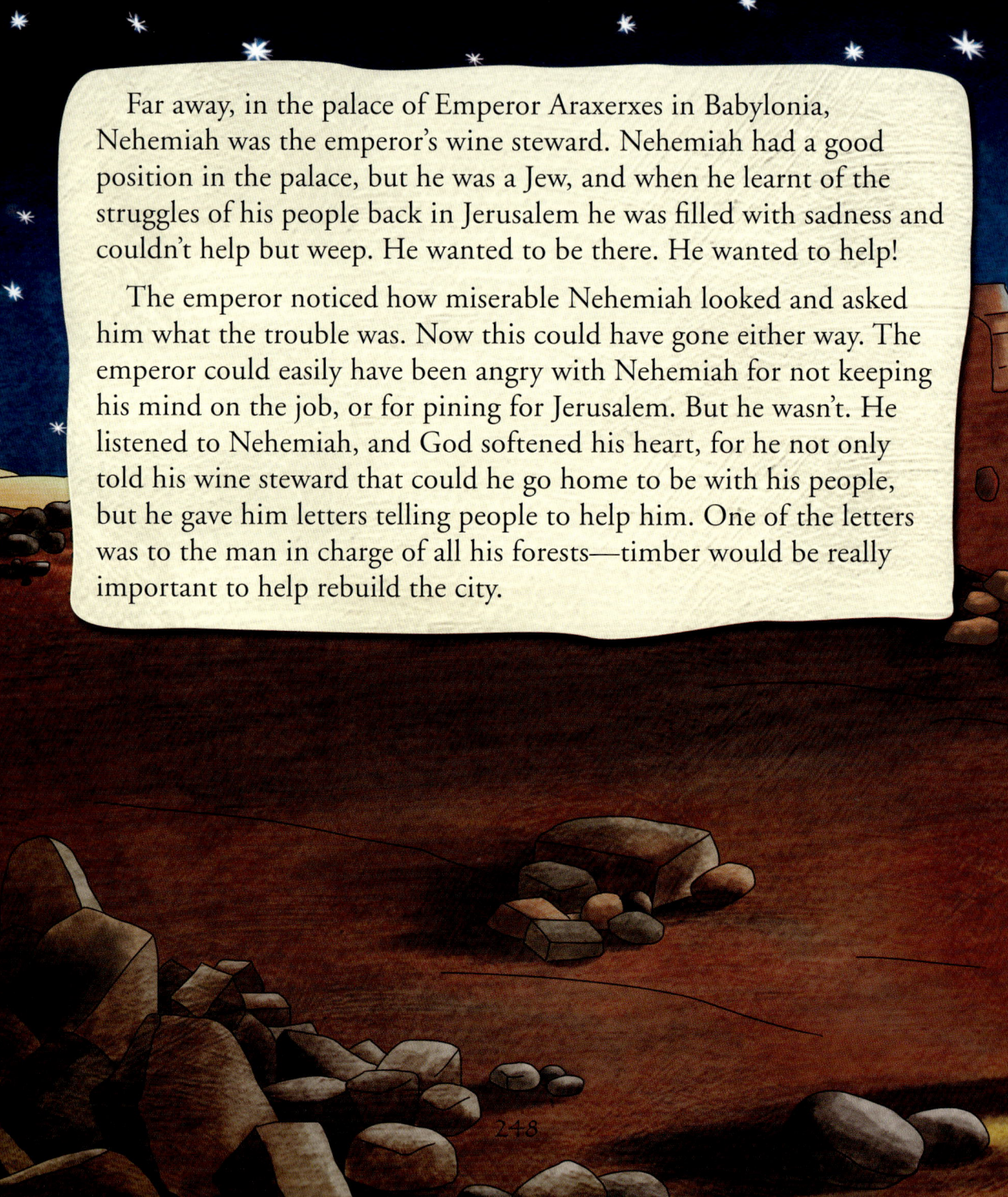

Far away, in the palace of Emperor Araxerxes in Babylonia, Nehemiah was the emperor's wine steward. Nehemiah had a good position in the palace, but he was a Jew, and when he learnt of the struggles of his people back in Jerusalem he was filled with sadness and couldn't help but weep. He wanted to be there. He wanted to help!

The emperor noticed how miserable Nehemiah looked and asked him what the trouble was. Now this could have gone either way. The emperor could easily have been angry with Nehemiah for not keeping his mind on the job, or for pining for Jerusalem. But he wasn't. He listened to Nehemiah, and God softened his heart, for he not only told his wine steward that could he go home to be with his people, but he gave him letters telling people to help him. One of the letters was to the man in charge of all his forests—timber would be really important to help rebuild the city.

The first thing that Nehemiah did when he returned to Jerusalem was to take a trip around the city walls to see just how bad things were. And let's be clear—things were really, really bad! Hardly any of the wall was still standing, and in some places there was so much rubble on the ground that his donkey couldn't get passed.

The next morning he gathered together the leaders of the people. "This is pathetic!" he declared. "You should be ashamed of yourselves! We need to rebuild the walls and make new gates. And we need to do it now! God helped me to get back here, and I know he will help us with the work! But let's get started right away!"

Nehemiah's coming filled the people with new energy. Everyone helped out with the building work.

But the Samaritans were far from pleased. They didn't want Jerusalem to be strong and safe behind big, sturdy walls. And so they tried to discourage their neighbours. "You'll never get it done!" they taunted. "You're wasting your time! Maybe you think you can pray to your God and he will put the walls up by magic for you—you'd better hope so! Because you'll never do it yourselves!"

But the Jews just put their heads down and ignored the taunts. They had more important things to do than listen to insults.

The Samaritans became worried. Maybe these Jews would actually get the wall built after all! They weren't going to let that happen. They planned an attack.

But Nehemiah knew what they were plotting. He wasn't going to let this halt their work. He knew that God wanted them to plough ahead, and he knew that God would look after them. He told every man to carry weapons, and he divided them into two groups—one group would work while the other stood guard.

Every day they began work when the first glimmer of the sun could be glimpsed over the horizon, and they were still working when the stars appeared in the night sky.

They worked, and worked, and worked … and in fifty-two days the walls were finished and Jerusalem was protected!

Starting Over

When all the building work was finished, the Israelites wanted to turn their mind to something even more important—their covenant with God.

They asked the prophet Ezra to bring out the Book of Law which God had given to Moses so long ago. Everyone gathered to listen to him—everyone who was old enough to listen and to understand. They all praised God and bowed down, and then he began. And to make sure that everyone understood, priests moved through the crowd to explain things and make it easy for them to understand.

Many of the people began to cry. They realised how far they had moved from God, and they felt very sorry. God had loved them, and done so much for them, and they had forgotten all about him and become wrapped up in their own lives, just thinking about themselves. It made them feel really miserable.

But Ezra told them not to cry. "This is a special day," he said. "It is a day to be happy, not sad. Let's celebrate God's love! Have a party with lots of food and sweet drinks, and make sure to share with everyone."

God was pleased that his people had opened up their hearts to him again. They really felt bad about how they had let him down, and they truly wanted in their hearts to obey and love and honour him.

The Beauty Contest

Back in Persia there was a new king. His name was Xerxes and he was rather proud and vain. He threw an enormous party and invited all the important people so that he could impress them and show off his fine palace, and his extravagant feasts, and his beautiful wife …

But he hit a bit of a snag. You see, Queen Vashti was not overly impressed when her husband sent one of his servants to fetch her so that he could parade her before his guests. She probably didn't want to go anywhere near him or his friends—the party had been going on for days and the king and his guests had been working their way through his wine cellar! No thank you! She would stay right where she was, if you don't mind!

But of course, Xerxes did mind. He minded a lot. What good was a wife if she didn't come when he told her to? And how dare she show him up in front of all of his guests?

His advisors were on his side too. They definitely liked the idea of women doing what they were told. What if word got out and their own wives decided to disobey them when they got back home? And so they urged him to get rid of the queen, and send her away. And find a new one. One who would do as she was told!

So Xerxes sent Vashti away, and ordered his soldiers to search throughout the land and find the prettiest young girls and bring them back to the palace, so that he could choose between them.

Now, one of these girls was a lovely maiden named Esther. Actually, her real name was Hadassah. It was a Jewish name because she was an exile from Jerusalem. Her cousin Mordecai had brought her up and was like a father to her, and he had warned her not to tell the king that she was Jewish. He wasn't sure how it would go down at court. So Esther it was.

There were many pretty girls brought before the king, but Esther was the prettiest, and the king chose her above all the rest to be his queen.

One day around the same time, Mordecai happened to overhear a couple of guards whispering together by the palace gates. They were plotting to kill the king! Mordecai went straight to his cousin and told her about the wicked scheme, and she told the king in time for the guards to be caught.

The whole affair was carefully noted in the palace records—yet the king forgot to reward the man who had saved his life! But don't worry, it wasn't the end of the story, as you will find out in a little while …

Enemy of the People

King Xerxes had chosen a new queen. And now he chose a new prime minister. His name was Haman.

Haman thought very well of himself. And he expected everyone else to think very well of him too. When he passed through the streets he expected everyone to bow before him. And generally speaking they did—Haman was not the sort of man you wanted to make an enemy of.

But Mordecai wasn't going to bow down before him. Hadn't God told his people only to bow down to him? So when Haman passed by, Mordecai stayed just as he was.

Haman was livid. How dare this unimportant man—this nobody!—disrespect him like that! When he found out that Mordecai was a Jew he determined to wreak revenge not only on Mordecai, but on all his people!

Haman was nothing if not cunning. He went to the king and slyly told him that he had learnt that there was a race of people living in his kingdom who refused to honour the king properly. They kept their own laws and didn't obey the king's laws. "It just isn't right," he argued. "They shouldn't be allowed to carry on like that! You should have them wiped out!"

The king agreed, and signed a decree stamped with the royal seal (one of those ones that can't be overturned or changed—remember Darius and Daniel?). The decree said that on the thirteenth day of the twelfth month of that year, all the Jewish people living in the empire should be killed—old and young, men and women, and even little children too! Messengers carried copies of this law to all corners of Persia.

When Mordecai found out about the dreadful decree he dressed himself in sackcloth and sat outside the palace gates and wept. When news of this reached Esther, she sent one of her servants to speak to him. And he brought back a very scary message. Mordecai wanted Esther to speak to the king and beg for mercy!

The Brave Queen

Now, we've already established that King Xerxes was not the most tolerant of rulers. Ask Queen Vashti what *she* thought! In fact, he had this thing going where if anyone came to see him without being sent for then they would be killed—unless he held out his golden scepter! So you can see why Esther wasn't keen on going to see him uninvited!

But Mordecai sent another message. "Don't you realise how many people will die? You probably feel pretty safe inside your palace, but what about those on the outside? And anyway, have you stopped to think why you're queen? Maybe God made you queen precisely so you could help his people!"

This was tough for Esther to hear. She was really scared. But she wanted to be brave for God! And in the end, she made up her mind to go and see the king.

She dressed herself in her finest clothes and put her hair up just the way the king liked it, yet when she walked up to the throne Esther was trembling with fear. But then Xerxes smiled at her and held out his golden scepter, and she heaved a sigh of relief (very discretely!)

"What did you want to ask me, Queen Esther," he said pleasantly. "I will give you anything you want—even half my kingdom!" (Clearly he was in a very good mood!)

Esther didn't want to spill the beans there in the throne room, with everyone listening. Instead, she invited the king and Haman to a banquet in her rooms, later that day.

Things went pretty well. The king certainly seemed to be enjoying himself, and seemed very happy to give her anything she wanted. But still Esther couldn't bring herself to tell him what the problem was. So she invited him and the prime minister to another feast, the next day! The king was happy to oblige, and Haman felt really pleased with himself, wining and dining with the king and queen!

But by the time Haman came to the meal the next day he was not feeling quite so happy. A sequence of events had really rocked his boat. First, he had decided to hang that irritating Mordecai who was still refusing to bow to him. He had even had the gallows built!

But in the meantime the king had happened to make a bit of a discovery. He had had trouble getting to sleep, and had been looking at the palace records (usually guaranteed to make him dose off!). But instead of sending him to sleep the records had reminded him of Mordecai's role in saving his life.

The king had sent for his prime minister, and had asked him what was the best way to honour somebody. Haman had instantly assumed that the king wanted to honour him, so he suggested a huge parade, with the honoured man riding the king's own horse and wearing the king's own robe. And as a special touch, Haman suggested that someone very important should be the one to lead the horse through the city.

Imagine Haman's emotions when he learnt that the man the king wanted to honour was Mordecai! And he was even more miserable when the king told him that he should be the one to lead the horse!

So, you can guess how furious the prime minister was by the time he reached Esther's rooms. And things were only going to get worse…

This time when the king asked her what it was that she wanted, Esther was brave enough to reply, "Please save me! And please save my people! Someone has plotted against us and we are to be wiped out completely!"

"Who would do such a dreadful thing?" asked the king incredulously.

"Our enemy is Haman!" replied the queen, and she pointed to the prime minister!

Xerxes was furious. So furious that he ordered that Haman should be hung on the very gallows he had built for Mordecai!

Saved!

Since the first law could not be changed or cancelled, Xerxes had Mordecai send out a new decree, and this one stated that all Jews had a right to arm themselves, and could fight back if attacked, and destroy their enemies.

So it was that on the thirteenth day of the twelfth month of that year, when the followers of Haman tried to massacre the Jews, the Jews fought back and defeated them throughout the empire!

And every year the Jewish people celebrate the holy festival of Purim, and remember how God saved them, through the bravery of Esther and Mordecai.

Jonah and the Very Big Fish

God had told Jonah to go to Nineveh. He wanted him to give a very important message to the people there. He wanted him to tell them to stop doing all the bad things that they were doing.

So Jonah got on a ship. Heading for Tarshish. And if you are wondering if Tarshish is on the way to Nineveh, it's not. It was in completely the wrong direction. About two and a half thousand miles in the wrong direction!

The problem was, Jonah really didn't like the Assyrians (Nineveh was in Assyria). They really didn't get along with the Jews. He thought they were bad people. And he thought they deserved everything that was coming to them! They should be punished! And he didn't want to be the one giving them a lifeline! He knew what would happen—they would repent, and because God is merciful and compassionate and loving he would forgive them. And Jonah didn't want him to forgive them!

So he was heading for Tarshish. He was running away!

The thing is, you really can't run away from God. It doesn't matter how far you go, he'll still be there. And Jonah should have known that.

He fell fast asleep on the ship as it headed in the wrong direction. A storm blew up—a dreadful storm. The ship rocked and rolled in the frothy waters, and waves slammed over the sides. The sailors were panic-stricken. "Someone on board must have angered one of the gods!" they wailed (they weren't Jews). "We're all going to die!"

They gathered everyone together and made them draw straws. They wanted to know who it was who had got them into this mess (sailors are a superstitious bunch!).

Jonah pulled the short straw. He wasn't surprised. He knew in his heart that God had sent this storm because of him.

"It's my fault," he owned up above the roar of the waves. "I tried to run away from God and he is angry with me. You should throw me overboard, and then the rest of you will be safe!"

The sailors threw up their hands in horror. No way were they going to toss him into that seething mass of water! But the ship began to creak and they were terrified that it would begin to break up beneath their feet.

"Trust me," said Jonah. "It's the only thing to do."

Reluctantly the sailors cast Jonah overboard. The second that he sank into the inky waters, the moment that he disappeared beneath the foamy crests of the waves, the storm ceased. It didn't die down. It just stopped. Instantly. And the sailors were filled with awe, and began to praise Jonah's God and to thank him for saving them.

As for Jonah, well, he sank slowly, inexorably down, down through the water. He had given himself into the hands of God and was resigned to his fate, so it must have come as a bit of a shock when all of a sudden a huge shape appeared before him, and as he tried to focus, he made out a huge mouth with huge teeth! And before he knew it, he had been swallowed by some enormous fish! Swallowed whole!

Deep inside the belly of the fish everything was dark (and probably rather smelly given all the rotten seaweed and fishbones around!) But Jonah was alive.

For three days and three nights Jonah sat inside the fish. He had plenty of time to think about what he had done. Plenty of time to realise how silly he had been. And plenty of time to want to put it right.

After three days the fish spat Jonah safely out onto shore. As he sat there, dripping wet (and smelly!), thinking about what had happened, God spoke to him again.

"Go to Nineveh, Jonah. Give them my message," he said.

And do you know what? This time Jonah was only too happy to do exactly as he was told! And the people of Nineveh heard God's message and were sorry, and God forgave them.

Let's not try to run away from God when he has something that he wants us to do. Let's be his messenger and bring his Word to everyone we know!

A Messenger is Coming

Years passed. Back in Jerusalem the returned exiles had started off so well. They had been full of good intentions. They wouldn't let God down again!

But slowly, inexorably, they forgot about their promises. They forgot to be thankful and started to moan. God sent another prophet to speak to them.

"You keep complaining that God isn't blessing you," Malachi told them. "But you have stopped loving him!

"God is going to send another messenger one day. A very special messenger, who will prepare the way for him. He will be like a scouring soap, a blazing fire, that burns away everything that is bad and leaves only what is pure. One day God's judgement will come on each and every one of us. If you obey him, then his power will shine on you like the lovely warm rays of the sun! So remember to obey him and love him with all your heart!"

Many, many years later someone else—like Jonah—would find themselves shut away in a dark place for three days and three nights. That someone would bring a message from God, too. A message for every single one of us.

That someone would be the most important messenger of all—the messenger that Malachi had spoken about!

And the next part of the story is all about him!

A Visit by an Angel

Mary lived in the village of Nazareth, halfway between the Sea of Galilee and the Mediterranean Sea. Not much went on in Nazareth, for it was small and unimportant, but Mary was happy and excited, for she was engaged to be married to Joseph, a carpenter who could trace his family back to King David.

Now, one day, Mary was quietly going about her chores when suddenly she was aware of a bright light shining before her, and she looked up to see an angel of God, all in white. She gasped in shock—what could this mean? But the angel smiled at her and said gently, "Mary, don't be afraid. God loves you and has blessed you. He has chosen you for a very special honour. You will give birth to a baby boy, and you are to call him Jesus. He will be called the Son of God, and his kingdom will never end!"

Mary was filled with wonder. "How can this be?" she asked softly. "I'm not even married!"

"Nothing is impossible for God," replied the angel. "The Holy Spirit will come on you, and your child will be God's own Son."

Mary could hardly believe what she was hearing, but she trusted God with all her heart. If he said it would happen, it would happen.

"I am God's servant," she said. "I'll do whatever God wants me to."

God spoke to Joseph in a dream and explained that Mary had not been unfaithful to him and that the child would be very special indeed. Joseph married Mary straight away and took good care of her.

An Important Journey

Soon it would be time for Mary to have her baby. She probably wanted to be nice and comfortable in her own home, with all her own things around her and her family nearby to help out. But that wasn't how it worked out.

You see, at exactly this time, the Emperor of Rome decided to order a census. The Emperor was a very powerful man and he ruled over many, many lands. He wanted to keep track of every single person in all the lands that he ruled over. He wanted to make sure that everyone paid their taxes! And so all the people throughout the lands ruled by Rome had to go to their hometown to be counted.

It so happened that Joseph's family was descended from King David, and so he and Mary had to travel to Bethlehem, where King David had been born. Mary's baby was due to be born any day, and the journey was long and hard, but, like everyone else, they had to do as the Emperor ordered.

When Mary and Joseph finally arrived in Bethlehem, they were tired and desperately wanted to find a room for the night, for the time had come for Mary's baby to be born.

But the town was filled to bursting, for everyone had come to be counted. The houses were crowded as families squeezed in, and as for the inns, well, every single room in every single inn was full. By the time that Joseph and Mary arrived in Bethlehem, there was nowhere for them to stay!

Things seemed very bleak, but at last, one kind innkeeper took pity on them.

"I'm afraid I have no rooms free, but if you don't mind a bit of straw, then I do have somewhere that you can spend the night," he said, and he showed them to a stable where the animals were kept. It was dirty and smelly, but it was the best they could do.

That night, Mary's baby was born. She wrapped him in strips of cloth, then laid him gently on clean straw in a manger—one of the troughs that the animals used for feeding. Mary and Joseph looked down upon their son with joy, and they named him Jesus, just as the angel had told them to.

And so, one of the prophesies of the Old Testament was fulfilled, for over seven hundred years before this, the prophet Isaiah had foretold that one day God would send a sign: "A young virgin will fall pregnant and will give birth to a son and will call him Immanuel."

You see, Immanuel means 'God is with us', and that is exactly what had happened—God had come to live with us on earth. Jesus was Immanuel!

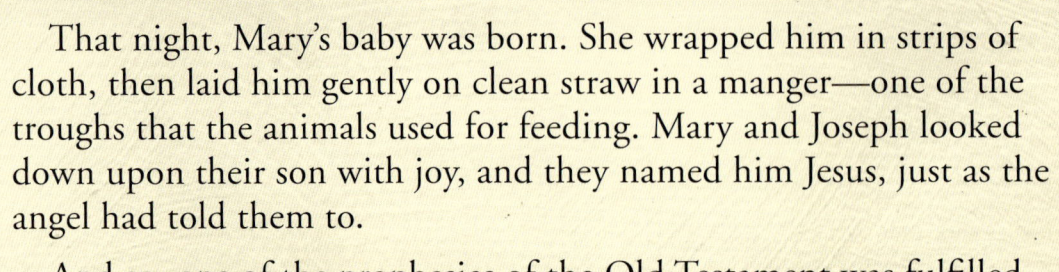

The Very First Visitors

That same night, on a hillside overlooking Bethlehem, some shepherds were watching over their sheep. Apart from keeping an eye out for wild animals, there wasn't much to do, so they sat around a fire sharing stories.

All of a sudden, the dark night sky was ablaze with light, and the shepherds fell to the ground in fright as an angel of the Lord appeared in the sky above them.

"Don't be afraid," the angel said to them gently, just as he had reassured Mary so many months ago. "I am here to bring you good news—the best news! Today a very special baby has been born in King David's town—he is Christ, the Messiah, God's own Son! Go and see for yourselves. You will find him lying in a manger in a stable."

And with these words the sky was filled with more angels, all singing a wonderful, beautiful song praising God: "Glory to God in the highest heaven, and peace on earth and good will to all men!"

And then, as swiftly as they had come, the angels disappeared.

In the silence that followed, the shepherds looked at one another in amazement. Had that really just happened? Had a host of shining angels just appeared to them, a bunch of dirty, raggedy shepherds?

But they didn't waste much time thinking about 'why?' for they were far too busy racing down to the town and searching for the stable where they would find the special baby. And when they did find Mary and Joseph, and little Jesus lying in the manger just as they had been told, their hearts exploded with joy and gratitude, and they rushed off to tell everyone they could find about the wonderful news.

Following a Star

In a distant land far to the east, three wise men had been studying the stars. These men were clever and respected and wealthy—you might even have mistaken them for kings if you had seen them in all their finery!

Anyway, one night they discovered a bright new star shining in the skies. They knew that it meant something very special—they knew that it was a sign that a great king had been born—and so they prepared for a long journey, packed up their things and followed the star all the way to Jerusalem.

In Jerusalem they made their way to the court of Herod the Great (who wasn't really so great, for he was actually rather cruel and wicked), who was the king of Judea (although really he had to do what the Roman Emperor told him to do). There they asked if he could show them the way to the baby who would be the king of the Jews.

Herod was horrified! He was king—he didn't want another king around! His advisors told him of a prophecy that the new king would be born in the city of King David, in Bethlehem.

Then the cunning king sent the wise men to Bethlehem, saying, "Once you have found him, come back and tell me where he is so that I can visit him too!" Mind you, he didn't say what sort of visit he wanted to pay him!

The wise men followed the star all the way to a humble house. There they found Jesus and his parents. Though he was only a little child, these wise and powerful men knelt down before him, and presented him with fine gifts of gold, sweet-smelling frankincense, and a spicy ointment called myrrh before returning home. But they did not stop off at Herod's palace, for God had warned them in a dream not to go there.

When King Herod realised that they weren't coming back he was furious. He was so angry that he gave an order that every boy under the age of two in Bethlehem should be killed. He wasn't taking any chances!

But no sooner had the wise men left Bethlehem than an angel appeared to Joseph in a dream. "You must take Mary and Jesus and set off at once for Egypt," warned the angel. "You are in danger here, for Herod will be sending soldiers to search for the child and kill him."

Joseph awoke with a start. He and Mary swiftly gathered their belongings, lifted little Jesus gently from his sleep, and set off in haste that very night on the long journey to Egypt, where they lived until wicked King Herod died. Then they came back to Nazareth once more, and as the years passed, Jesus grew to be filled with grace and wisdom and kindness.

Cousin John

Now, shortly before Jesus came into the world, another special baby was born. His name was John, and his parents were Zechariah and Elizabeth, who was Mary's cousin. Elizabeth and Zechariah were very old when John was born, so he was a wonderful gift from God, and God had a very special plan for him, for John was to prepare the way for Jesus.

When John grew up, he went to live in the desert. He wore clothes made of smelly camels' hair and lived on dry, crunchy locusts and wild honey! To be honest, he was rather strange, but nevertheless, people came from all around to listen to what he had to say, for his words rang true. "Be sorry for your sins, and God will forgive you. And get ready in your hearts, for your King is coming soon!" John would tell them. It wasn't enough for them to carry on the way they were—they needed to repent and change their ways. Many truly were sorry, and if they were, John took them down to the River Jordan, and there he would baptise them in the water as a sign that all their sins had been washed away and that they could start a new life.

People began to wonder if maybe John was the one that the prophets had spoken about so many years ago, the promised King, but he told them, "I'm baptising you with water, but the one who will come after me will baptise you with the Holy Spirit and with fire! I'm not even worthy to tie up his sandals!"

One day, John was by the river when Jesus came to him. As soon as he saw him, John knew who this special person was. Here was the holy 'Lamb of God'! Which made him all the more shocked when Jesus asked John to baptise him!

"You can't be serious!" he protested uncomfortably. "I shouldn't be baptising you—I should be begging you to baptise me!"

But Jesus just smiled and told him that this was what God wanted, and so John took him into the river.

At the very moment that Jesus came up out of the water, the heavens opened and the skies shone brightly and, like a dove, the Holy Spirit rested on Jesus. Then a voice came from above, "This is my Son, and I love him. I am very pleased with him."

At last, the much longed-for King had come to save his people!

The Big Test

It was nearly time for Jesus to start spreading God's message to his people, but first of all, there was something he had to do.

The Holy Spirit led Jesus into the desert. It was dusty and stony and dry, and it was baking hot during the day. For forty days Jesus stayed in the desert, and in all that time he ate no food. Can you imagine that? By the end of that time he was very hungry indeed!

Then the devil came to test him—just as he had tested Adam and Eve in the Garden of Eden so many, many years before—saying, "If you're really the Son of God, surely you can do anything. Why don't you just tell these stones to become bread? How hard would that be?"

Jesus wasn't Adam. He answered calmly, "It says in the Scriptures, 'Man shall not live on bread alone, but on every word that comes from the mouth of God.'"

He knew that food wasn't the most important thing in life.

Not to be put off, the devil took Jesus to the top of a temple and told him to throw himself off. "If you're the Son of God, surely his angels would rescue you?" he taunted.

But Jesus said, "It is also written: 'Do not put the Lord your God to the test.'"

The devil tried yet again to tempt Jesus. He took him to the very top of a high mountain and showed him the land that stretched for miles and miles in every direction. "All you have to do is bow down and worship me, and I will give you all the kingdoms of the world!" he coaxed.

But Jesus replied, "Go away, Satan! For it is written: 'Worship the Lord your God, and serve only him.'"

When the devil finally realised that he could not tempt Jesus, he gave up in disgust and left him there in the desert, and God sent his angels to Jesus to help him recover.

Now it was time for Jesus to truly start his work on earth.

Jesus' Special Friends

Simon sat on the gently swaying boat, looking up at the man who stood talking by his side, and beyond him to the crowd of people on the shore, listening eagerly to what he had to say.

Today had not been like any other day. Simon had been mending his nets by the shore when a man had come to the lake and had begun speaking. Slowly but surely the crowds had gathered to listen to this man—Jesus, he was called—talk about God's love and forgiveness, and explain the Scriptures in a way that seemed so different from the way the priests talked in the synagogues. When Jesus spoke, everything seemed clear.

But so many people came to listen that it was difficult for everyone to hear what Jesus was saying, and so Jesus had turned to Simon and had asked him if he wouldn't mind taking him out on his fishing boat, so that people could see him more clearly. And now, along with the crowd, Simon drank in every word he had to say.

Afterwards, when the crowd had dispersed, Jesus told Simon to push the boat out farther into the water and let down his nets. "Master," Simon answered, "we were out all night and didn't catch a thing. But if you say so, then we will try again."

He couldn't believe his eyes when he pulled up his nets full of fish! He called to his brother, Andrew, and to his friends James and John to help, and soon the two boats were so full of fish that they were nearly ready to sink!

Simon fell to his knees in wonder, but Jesus smiled. "Don't be afraid, Simon. From now on you shall be called Peter (the Greek word for 'rock') for that is what you will be."

Then Jesus turned to all the men. "I want you to leave your nets," he said, "and come with me and fish for men instead, so that we can spread the good news!"

The four men had been fishermen all their life—nets and tides, fish and sails were all they knew—yet they pulled their boats up on the beach, left everything behind, and followed Jesus without a backward glance!

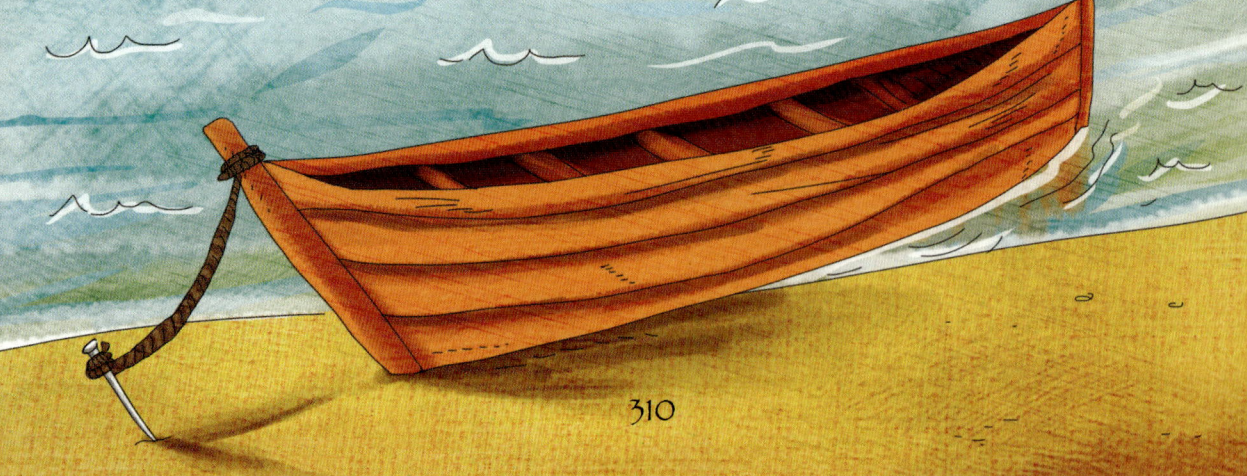

These were the first special friends that Jesus called to help him in his work, but they weren't the last. Over time, Jesus chose twelve men to be his disciples, to pass on his message of good news, and to be there, after his death, to carry on his work. They weren't all fishermen—there was also a tax collector, Matthew, who left his well-paid job on the spot when Jesus told him to follow him. Not everybody was thrilled when Jesus became friendly with Matthew, for people thought that tax collectors were greedy and dishonest. But Jesus told them, "If you go to a doctor's surgery, you don't expect to see healthy people—it's people who are sick who need to see the doctor. I am God's doctor. I have come here to save those people who are sinners and who want to start afresh. Those who have done nothing wrong don't need me!"

As well as the fishermen and Matthew, Jesus called another Simon, a patriot who wanted to fight the Romans, and six more men: Bartholomew, Thomas, James son of Alphaeus, Philip, Judas (or Thaddeus) son of James, and Judas Iscariot.

Jesus knew they would have a hard task ahead of them. He wanted them to teach the people that God's kingdom is near, and to heal people too. Later on, these men became known as apostles, or messengers, for they were chosen especially by Jesus to pass on his message of good news.

Water into Wine

Not long after Jesus had called Simon Peter and the other fishermen to follow him, he was invited to a marvellous wedding party along with his friends and his mother. Everyone was having a wonderful time—the music was cheerful, the food was delicious, and the wine was . . . Actually, everything was going well until the wine ran out!

Mary rushed to tell Jesus, who asked her, "Why are you telling me this? It is not yet time for me to show myself." But Mary still hoped he would help, and spoke quietly to the servants, telling them to do whatever Jesus told them to.

There were several huge water jars nearby. Jesus told the servants to fill them with water, and then pour the water into jugs and take it to the headwaiter to taste. When the headwaiter tasted it, he was amazed. He exclaimed to the bridegroom, "Most people serve the best wine at the start of a meal, but you have saved the best till last!" for the jugs were now filled with delicious wine!

This was the first of many miracles which Jesus would perform.

The Healer

Jesus travelled from town to town with his friends, spreading his message. One day he was walking through a village when a man came up to him and fell to his knees in front of him. "Sir," he begged, looking humbly up at Jesus, "If you want to, you can make me clean."

The people around Jesus edged back in fear and disgust. The man in front of them was a leper—he was suffering from a dreadful skin disease and was wrapped in bandages. He even smelt! Worse than that, they were worried that they might catch the disease too.

But Jesus was filled with compassion. He reached out and touched the man gently. "I do want to," he said. "Be clean!"

And no sooner had he spoken than the man's skin was smooth and clear and healthy. People could hardly believe their eyes!

Jesus said to the man, "Don't tell anyone about this. Go straight to the priest and let him examine you."

But the grateful man simply couldn't keep the wonderful event to himself, and before long so many people wanted to come and see Jesus that he could no longer go anywhere without being surrounded by crowds. Now, wherever Jesus went, people would flock to see him, not just to listen to all the amazing things he had to tell them, but also for healing—for themselves or for their friends and family.

One time, some men brought their friend to the house where Jesus was staying. They hoped Jesus would heal him. Their friend was paralysed and couldn't walk, so they carried him between them on a makeshift stretcher. When they got there, the house was so crowded they couldn't get in—they couldn't even get close to the front door! But the men weren't going to give up that easily. Instead, they climbed up onto the roof, made a hole in it and then lowered their friend down through it on a mat!

When Jesus saw how strongly they believed in him, he spoke kindly to the man, saying, "Your sins are forgiven, my friend." Jesus knew what was truly important.

But among the people inside the house were several teachers of the law. They were very offended when they heard Jesus say this. This was outrageous! Who did he think he was? Only God could forgive sin!

Jesus knew exactly what they were thinking. He turned to them and said calmly, "Do you think it's easier to say to this man, 'Your sins are forgiven,' or to say, 'Get up and walk'? The Son of Man has authority on earth to forgive sins."

Then he turned back to the man and said, "Get up now. Pick up your mat, and go home," and the man stood up, picked up the mat, and walked straight out the front door! Everyone was filled with wonder.

The Sermon on the Mount

For many people, the words that Jesus spoke healed them deep within. More and more people wanted to listen to this wonderful man—but the priests and teachers of the law weren't always so pleased to have him around. They felt that he was stepping on their toes and saying things that he had no right to say. They wanted people to listen to them, not him! All too often, Jesus wasn't made welcome in the synagogues, so sometimes he would teach his disciples and the large crowds which gathered to hear him outside in the open air. One of the most important talks he gave was on a mountain near Capernaum. It has become known as the Sermon on the Mount. Jesus taught the people about what was truly important in life and gave them comfort and advice on how to live their lives.

He told them, "It is important to obey all of God's laws, but that isn't enough—you need to understand the meaning behind them. You need to learn to truly forgive people when they do something you don't like, or that hurts you. That is the way to get closer to God. It's easy to love those who love you, but I say, love your enemies! After all, God gives his sunlight and rain to both good and bad people!"

He told them that they should try to set a good example to others—"but don't just do good things in order to impress other people. You don't need anyone else's praise—God can see inside your hearts and he knows the truth! And always try to treat other people in the same way that you would like them to treat you. Don't judge them. Think about your own faults first!"

He offered them comfort as well. He told them that all those who were poor or sad, or who had lived a hard life would one day be happy in heaven. So too would all those who were kind and humble, all those who kept the peace and who tried to do the right thing. They would all be rewarded in heaven, so they must not give up hope, however hard things seemed.

"That is what you need to focus on—the end goal," he continued. "Don't store up wealth on earth. It won't last! Store up treasures in heaven, for where your treasures are, your heart will be too. Don't worry about what clothes you're wearing or where your next meal will come from. There is more to life than food and clothes. Look at the birds in the sky. They don't have to plant and harvest and store their food—God feeds them, doesn't he?

"And what about the beautiful wild flowers that grow everywhere? They don't have to work hard either, for God himself clothes them, and how splendid they look dressed in all their wonderful colours! And, if God cares for the birds and the flowers, don't you think he loves you even more? So trust him to look after you!"

Jesus also taught people the right way to pray. They shouldn't try to impress others by praying in public, but should go to a quiet place and pray to God alone. Nor should they keep repeating meaningless words. God knows what is in our hearts, and this is the way Jesus told people to pray to him:

> Our Father in heaven,
> Hallowed be your name.
> Your kingdom come.
> Your will be done,
> on earth as it is in heaven.
> Give us today our daily bread,
> and forgive us our sins,
> as we forgive those who sin against us.
> Lead us not into temptation,
> but deliver us from evil.
> For yours is the kingdom,
> the power and the glory, forever.
> Amen.

"Keep on asking," said Jesus, "and you will receive. Keep on seeking, and you will find. Keep on knocking, and the door will be opened to you."

Before Jesus ended his sermon, he said one last thing: "If you listen to my teaching and follow it then you are wise, like the person who builds his house on solid rock. Even if the rain pours down, the rivers flood, and the winds rage, the house won't collapse for it is built on solid rock.

"But if you listen and don't obey then you are foolish, like a person who builds a house on sand, without any foundations. The house might be built very quickly, but when the rains and floods and winds come, the house won't be able to stand against them. It will collapse and be completely destroyed."

As the crowds slowly dispersed, their heads were filled with all these new ideas. Jesus was nothing like their usual teachers, but what he said made sense. They had a lot to think about!

The Man Who Amazed Jesus

One day, Jesus was in Capernaum. He spent a lot of his time in this small fishing town, on the banks of the Sea of Galilee. This was where he had met Simon Peter and the others, and where Matthew used to collect taxes.

In Capernaum there lived a Roman officer. Romans didn't normally get on well with the Jews, but this officer was a good man, who treated the Jews well. He was also kind to the people who worked for him in his house, and that was why, when he heard that Jesus was in Capernaum, he came to ask for his help, for one of his servants was very ill.

"Lord," the officer said to Jesus, "my servant is very sick. He can't get out of bed, and he is suffering awfully. I am ever so fond of him, but I'm afraid he is close to death."

Jesus asked him, "Shall I come and heal him?"

But the officer replied, "Lord, I don't deserve to have you come to my own house! I am not worthy of that! But I know that you don't need to anyway. If you just say the word, I know that my servant will be healed, just in the same way that when I order my soldiers to do something, they do it!" The officer believed in Jesus so much that he didn't even need him to visit the sick man himself!

Jesus was amazed. He said to the people around him, "I've never come across faith like this before!" Then he turned back to the officer, saying, "Go home now, and what you believe will be done for you."

So the officer returned to his house, and sure enough, when he arrived back home, he found his servant up on his feet and feeling perfectly well again!

Jesus Calms the Storm

It was a beautiful evening. Peter and John and the other disciples were in a small fishing boat, heading happily over the Sea of Galilee. Jesus had spent all day by the lake, talking to people about God's message. People had come from far and wide to hear what he had to say, and to listen to his wonderful stories about God's love and forgiveness, and now Jesus was tired out. In fact, the minute he had lain down in the boat, he had fallen fast asleep!

The waters were calm and peaceful, and small waves lapped against the side of the boat and ruffled the sails as the friends chatted quietly about the day's events. Suddenly, the skies above darkened as clouds rolled in above them. A fierce storm struck the lake, the wind howled angrily, and huge waves tossed the boat from side to side.

The friends jumped up to reef the sails but could hardly keep their footing as the boat lurched violently and water poured into it. Lightning lit up the dark sky, and thunder echoed overhead. Some of the disciples were fishermen. They had sailed on these waters all their lives—the Sea of Galilee was known for its sudden squalls and raging storms—but never had they seen a storm as terrible and as terrifying as this one! They could hardly hear themselves think for the roar of the wind and the hammering of the rain, and they feared that at any moment their small boat could capsize.

Yet through it all, Jesus slept peacefully in the stern!

"Master, Master!" cried the frightened disciples. "Wake up and save us!"

Jesus opened his eyes and looked up at them. "Why are you so afraid?" he said sadly. "You have so little faith!"

Then he stood up calmly in the swaying boat and turned to face the wind and driving rain. "Be still," he said. That was all, nothing more. Just, "Be still."

And the storm was gone! The wind and the waves died down, the rain stopped and everything was calm once more.

The friends looked at one another. Something far more shocking than the storm had just happened. Who was this man who could speak to the wind and the waves—and be obeyed?! They did not yet understand the truth, that this was truly the Son of God, who would save them all.

So long as Jesus is with us, there is nothing to be afraid of. If he can calm the storms of the sea with just a couple of words, surely he can calm the storms of life as well.

Just Sleeping

Poor Jairus was in a dreadful state! His heart ached as he watched his wife wring her hands together in despair, for his little girl was terribly ill. She was only twelve years old, and was the light of their life, and nothing that they did seemed to make any difference. The doctors had given up hope. But Jairus hadn't. He had learnt that Jesus was in town and he had heard the rumours about all the wonderful things that he had done and all the people he had managed to cure. He was certain that all he needed to do was to get Jesus to come and see his daughter, and all would be well—but he knew he was running out of time!

When he found Jesus, surrounded by a multitude of people, he threw himself at his feet and begged him to come and help his little girl, for she was dying. Jesus helped Jairus to his feet, and promised that he would come immediately.

But people crowded around on all sides, everyone eager to see Jesus and to get close to him. Jairus' heart was pounding. He was so worried that they wouldn't get there in time.

And then his heart sank, for Jesus stopped still. "Who touched me?" he asked, looking around him.

"Master, everyone is touching you in this crowd!" said a disciple, but Jesus knew that he had been touched in a special way.

As he looked around, a woman stepped forward hesitantly and knelt at his feet. "Lord, it was me," she said nervously. For years she had been ill and nobody had been able to help her, but she had known that if she could just get close to Jesus, just touch him, she would be healed. And sure enough, the moment she had managed to touch the edge of his cloak, she was well again!

Jesus wasn't angry. "Your faith has made you well," he said kindly to the woman, smiling down at her. "Go home now and be at peace." And the woman left, full of gratitude and happiness.

But just then, someone came running up to Jairus. It was one of his servants. His face was grim, and Jairus didn't need to wait for him to speak to know that the news was bad. They were too late! Jairus' daughter was dead. Poor Jairus was heartbroken, but Jesus carried on walking. "Trust me, Jairus," he said. "Don't be afraid. Just believe."

When Jesus and Jairus arrived at the house, the air was filled with the sound of weeping. "Why are you carrying on so?" he asked. "The girl is not dead—she is just sleeping." The people there laughed at him bitterly, for they knew perfectly well that the child was dead. But Jesus ignored them and went into the house along with Peter and James and John, and Jairus and his wife. Everyone else he told to wait outside.

Then Jesus went to the room where the little girl lay on the bed, perfectly still. Tenderly taking one of her hands in his own, Jesus whispered, "Wake up, my child!"

In that instant, the child opened her eyes. She smiled at Jesus and hugged her overjoyed parents! Jesus told them to go and bring her some food, and he also told them not to talk about what had happened.

There is nothing that Jesus cannot do. Don't be afraid—just believe!

Special Stories

Many of the people who came to listen to Jesus were craftsmen or farmers, and many more kept animals or had their own vegetable garden. Jesus tried to pass on his message in a way that they would understand. He made up stories, often called parables, to let people think things through for themselves. To some they would just be stories, but others would understand the real message . . .

"A farmer went out to sow some seeds," said Jesus, looking at the bright and eager faces all around him. "As he was scattering it, some fell along the path and was trampled on, or eaten by birds. Some fell on rocky ground where there was no soil. When those seeds began to grow into little plants, they withered up and died almost straight away because their roots couldn't reach water. Other seeds fell among weeds which wrapped round them and choked them. But some seeds—a few—fell on good soil and grew into tall, strong, healthy plants and produced a wonderful crop, far greater than what was sown."

Jesus was telling them that he was like the farmer, and the seeds were like the message he brought from God. The seeds that fell on the path and were eaten by birds are like those people who hear the good news but pay no attention. Those that fell on the rocky ground are like people who are filled with joy when they first learn about the message, but don't have any roots, and so, while they believe for a while, when life gets difficult they give up easily. The seeds among weeds are like those people who hear but let themselves become overwhelmed and sidetracked by all of life's worries and pleasures. But the seeds that fell on good soil are like those people who hear God's message and hold it tight in their heart. Their faith grows and grows!

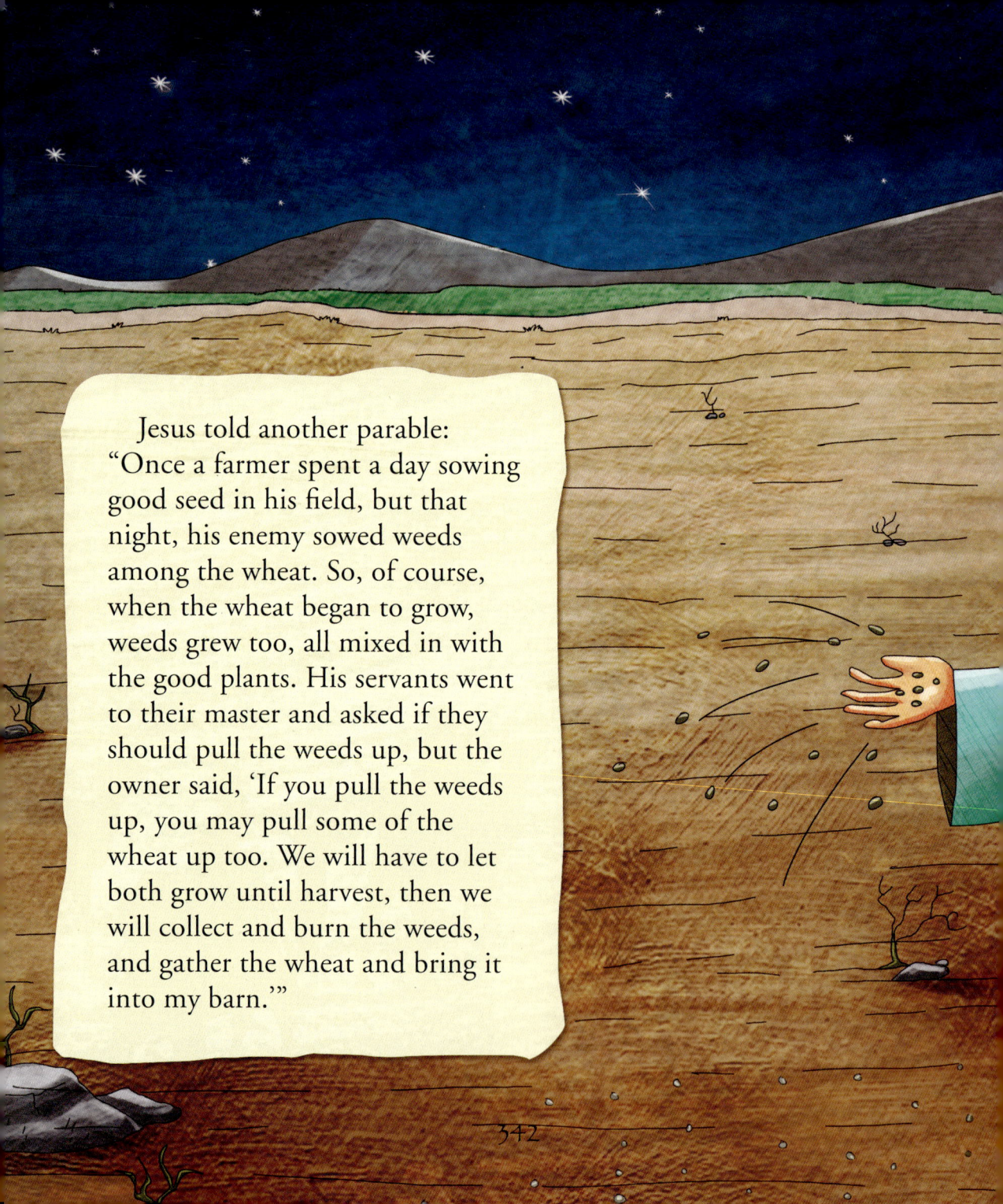

Jesus told another parable: "Once a farmer spent a day sowing good seed in his field, but that night, his enemy sowed weeds among the wheat. So, of course, when the wheat began to grow, weeds grew too, all mixed in with the good plants. His servants went to their master and asked if they should pull the weeds up, but the owner said, 'If you pull the weeds up, you may pull some of the wheat up too. We will have to let both grow until harvest, then we will collect and burn the weeds, and gather the wheat and bring it into my barn.'"

Later on that evening, the disciples asked Jesus what the story meant. Jesus explained, "The farmer who sowed the good seed is the Son of Man. The field is the world, and the good seed is the people of the kingdom. The weeds were sown by the devil, and they are his people. The harvest will come at the end of time. Then the Son of Man will send out his angels, and they will weed out of his kingdom everything that causes sin and all those people who do evil things and think evil thoughts and throw them into the blazing furnace. But those people who are good will shine as brightly as the sun in the kingdom of their Father."

If you have a vegetable garden, however carefully you look after it, and however many carrots and potatoes and peas and tomatoes you grow in it, there are probably some nasty weeds too. If we try to dig them out, we might dig out some of the good plants too. If we try to use weedkiller on them—well, most weedkillers don't know the difference between one plant and the next and will just kill everything! So sometimes, it is best to wait until harvest time, and then you can pull up and enjoy all your wonderful fruit and vegetables and throw the weeds on the bonfire!

In life, we can come across people who are like weeds in a garden. But it isn't our job to judge them—leave the weeds for God to take care of, and try to show love and kindness to all of his people.

The Mustard Seed and the Yeast

Jesus told his followers another parable: "The kingdom of heaven is like a mustard seed, which a man took and planted in the ground. Now, a mustard seed is tiny—in fact, it's the smallest of all seeds, but don't let that fool you, for when it grows, then it can grow bigger than all the other herbs, and become a tree, big enough that the birds can come and perch in its branches!"

Then he continued, "The kingdom of heaven is like yeast that a woman took and mixed into about sixty pounds of flour until it worked all through the dough." You see, you only need a very small amount of yeast to add to some flour and water and a bit of salt and sugar to make a lovely big loaf of bread. Sixty pounds of flour is quite a lot of flour, but you don't need lots of yeast. Just a small piece of yeast will have a huge effect.

Jesus was saying that we are never too small to be important in God's eyes, and that however little we are, we can help to grow the kingdom of God. From small beginnings can come wonderful things!

Hidden Treasure

Jesus was speaking to his disciples. Everyone else had gone home, but he had a special message for his friends: "The kingdom of heaven is like treasure hidden in a field," he told them. "Once there was a man who was digging in a field. He came upon a chest of buried treasure! When he opened it, it was full of gold coins and wonderful jewels that sparkled and shone in the sunlight. The man was so excited that he put the chest back in the ground and covered it up carefully with soil. Then he rushed off and sold his house and his land and everything he had, just so that he could buy that field and own the treasure himself!"

Jesus continued, "The kingdom of heaven is like a merchant on the lookout for beautiful pearls. He would travel the countryside in search of pearls. One day he came across one more beautiful than he had ever seen before. It was perfect! The merchant thought it was so precious that he sold everything he had so that he could buy this one pearl."

Jesus was talking about the most important thing of all—God's love. This love is the greatest treasure that we can possibly find. It is more precious than silver or gold or jewels—and absolutely worth giving everything else up for!

A Lamp on a Stand

Jesus wanted to explain how important it was for his followers to hear his message, take it to heart—and then to pass it on. He said to them, "No one lights a lamp and then covers it up with a bowl or hides it under a bed. Instead, they put the lamp on a stand so that anyone who comes in will see the light. Everything that is hidden will become clear, and everything that is secret will be brought out into the open."

He wanted them to think very carefully about what he was telling them so that they themselves could be lamps, shining forth in the world, bringing light into the lives of those around them. A light is made to be seen, it is made to be used—we must use what God has given us!

They weren't to keep his wonderful news a secret for themselves. They should share it, and in doing so would be filled with light. Jesus is the light of the world, and he came into it, not to stay hidden, but to light up the world with the truth about God. And when we let Jesus into our hearts, we shine too!

Five Loaves of Bread and Two Fish

News about Jesus and the wonderful stories that he told and things that he did spread throughout the land. Everywhere Jesus went he was surrounded by people.

One day, Jesus and his disciples had sailed across the lake to a quiet, remote place, away from the towns and cities, to spend some time alone. But the crowds had followed Jesus even there, and he could not bring himself to send them away, for they were like sheep without a shepherd, and his heart was filled with love and pity for them.

He spent all day talking, his words helping to set these people on the path towards his Father in heaven, and when evening fell the crowds were still there—around about five thousand of them! No one seemed to want to go home!

The disciples gathered around Jesus. "Master," said one, "what shall we do? Shouldn't we send these people off to find food for themselves? It's getting very late!"

"They don't need to go away," said Jesus. "Give them something to eat yourselves."

"But Master!" exclaimed the disciples, "we don't have any food to give them, and it would cost a fortune to go and buy food for them all!"

"What food do we have?" asked Jesus calmly, and after a frantic scrabbling around, the disciples came up with five loaves of bread and a couple of fish that one little boy happened to have for his dinner. Five loaves of bread and two fish—for five thousand people!

The disciples were rather bewildered, but Jesus simply told them to get the people to sit down on the grass in groups, and then he took the loaves of bread and the two fish, looked up to heaven and gave thanks to his Father, and broke the loaves into pieces. He gave them to the disciples, who put them in baskets and took them to the people and then came back to Jesus for more bread and fish. He filled up their baskets again . . . and again . . . and again! To their astonishment there was still bread and fish left in the baskets when they came to feed the very last people! More than five thousand people had been fed that day—with five loaves of bread and two fish!

You see, even when we don't have very much, if we give what we have to God and trust in him, he can do more with it than we could ever have imagined!

Walking on Water

It was late at night. All the crowds had finally gone home, and now the disciples were on their own in a fishing boat in the middle of the lake. Jesus had sent them on ahead of him to travel over to the other side of the lake, while he stayed behind to be alone and to pray on a quiet hillside.

But the disciples were worried. A sudden squall had come upon them. The wind howled furiously and waves tossed the boat violently and, row as hard as they could, they didn't seem to be getting anywhere fast. At the first light of dawn, they saw a figure walking towards them on the water! They were overcome with fear—was it a ghost? But then they heard the calm voice of Jesus saying, "It is I. Don't be afraid."

Simon Peter was the first to speak. "Lord," he said, "if it is really you, then order me to walk across the water to you."

Jesus answered Simon Peter and said, "Come."

Simon Peter put one foot gingerly in the water. Then he lowered the other, and bravely stood up, letting go of the boat. He didn't sink! But when he looked around at the waves, his courage failed him. As he began to sink, he cried out, "Lord, save me!"

Jesus reached out and took his hand. "Oh, Peter," he said sadly, "where is your faith? Why did you doubt?"

Then together they walked back to the boat. The wind died down, and the water became calm. The disciples bowed low. They were filled with awe and wonder. "You really are the Son of God!" they said humbly.

In our lives we will go through many storms. Keep your eyes on Jesus, and you will be safe.

On the Mountain Top

Jesus climbed up a mountain to pray, taking with him Peter, James and John. It was a wonderful place to stop and think in peace and quiet, and to see things clearly.

All of a sudden, as Jesus prayed, the disciples looked up to see him changed. Light shone from his face, and his clothes became whiter than anyone could wash them, dazzlingly white! As they watched in wonder, Moses, who had led his people out of Egypt, and Elijah, greatest of all the prophets, were suddenly there before their very eyes, talking with Jesus! Then a bright cloud covered them, and a voice said, "This is my own dear Son, whom I love. Listen to what he has to say, for I am very pleased with him!"

The disciples fell to the ground, too frightened to raise their eyes. But Jesus came over and touched them. "Don't be afraid," he said softly, and when they looked up, they saw no one there except Jesus.

When Jesus was on earth, there were lots of different ideas about who he really was. Some people thought that he was another prophet, or someone come back from the dead—Elijah maybe, or John the Baptist, who had been killed by King Herod. Others just thought he was a good teacher, and there were probably plenty of people who just thought he was rather strange!

But from that moment on, Peter, James, and John had no doubt at all about who Jesus was. He was the Son of God. God had said it, and that was that.

The Frantic Father

The very next day, when Jesus and his friends came down from the mountain, the other disciples came to meet them. They were surrounded by a large crowd, and out of the crowd a man called out in anguish, "Teacher, please look at my son! He is possessed by a demon, and he has dreadful fits. Sometimes he can't speak, or he is thrown to the ground and foams at the mouth! Please, please help him! I asked your disciples to help, but they couldn't drive the demon out."

Jesus looked at the disciples in disappointment. "Why don't you people believe? How long must I put up with you?" he said in sorrow. His disciples had seen so much, and had done so much, and yet they still didn't have the faith to heal this boy and cast out the bad spirit.

He told them to bring the young boy to him, and as soon as the boy came close to Jesus, the spirit threw the child to the ground, where he rolled around, foaming at the mouth uncontrollably.

"If you can really do anything, please help us!" begged the father.

"'If you can?'" repeated Jesus. "'*If?*' Don't you know that anything is possible for someone who truly believes?"

The father exclaimed, "I do believe! Help me believe more!"

Then Jesus commanded the spirit to come out, and the boy was healed. As simple as that!

Later that day, the disciples came to Jesus rather sheepishly and asked him why they hadn't been able to drive out the demon themselves, and he told them that they had needed to pray. Maybe this demon had been stronger than ones they had come across before. Maybe it had been harder to cast it out—and they had met this difficulty by worrying about whether they really could heal the boy, instead of turning to God and asking for his help, and continuing to have faith in what they knew was possible.

He told them, "The truth is, if you really do have faith, even if your faith is as small as a mustard seed, you can say to this mountain, 'Move from here to there,' and it will move. Nothing—absolutely nothing—will be impossible for you!"

The Good Neighbour

Once a lawyer asked Jesus a question. He wanted to know what Jesus thought he should do to be able to live forever in heaven. Jesus turned the question back on the man. "What do *you* think you should do?" he asked. "What does the law say?"

"'Love God with all your heart and all your soul,' and 'Love your neighbour just as you love yourself,'" replied the man rather smugly. After all, he was an expert in the law!

Jesus nodded. "You're right. If you do this, you will inherit eternal life." But he knew the man hadn't finished yet. He waited.

"So who exactly *is* my neighbour?" the lawyer duly continued. "Is it the couple who live in the next house to mine, or the people farther down the road?"

Jesus looked around at all the people. This was a very important thing to ask. When God had given Moses the special commandments so long ago, there had been two commandments which were more important than all the rest—"Love God with all your heart, and all your soul, and all your strength, and all your mind", and "Love your neighbour just as you love yourself,"—just as the lawyer had said. These commandments were so very important, because if people truly loved God and truly loved other people, then they would want to follow all the other commandments anyway.

But the man in the crowd had missed the point. Jesus wanted to explain just what God meant.

"Once there was a man who was travelling from Jerusalem to Jericho," Jesus began. The people who had gathered around him made themselves comfortable—Jesus was clearly going to tell one of his special stories!

"This man," continued Jesus, "was walking along the dusty road when all of a sudden some men jumped out from behind some rocks and began hitting him. They pushed him to the ground and kicked him, and then stole everything he had with him—his bag, his money, and even his clothes. They left him there in a ditch by the roadside and ran away into the hills.

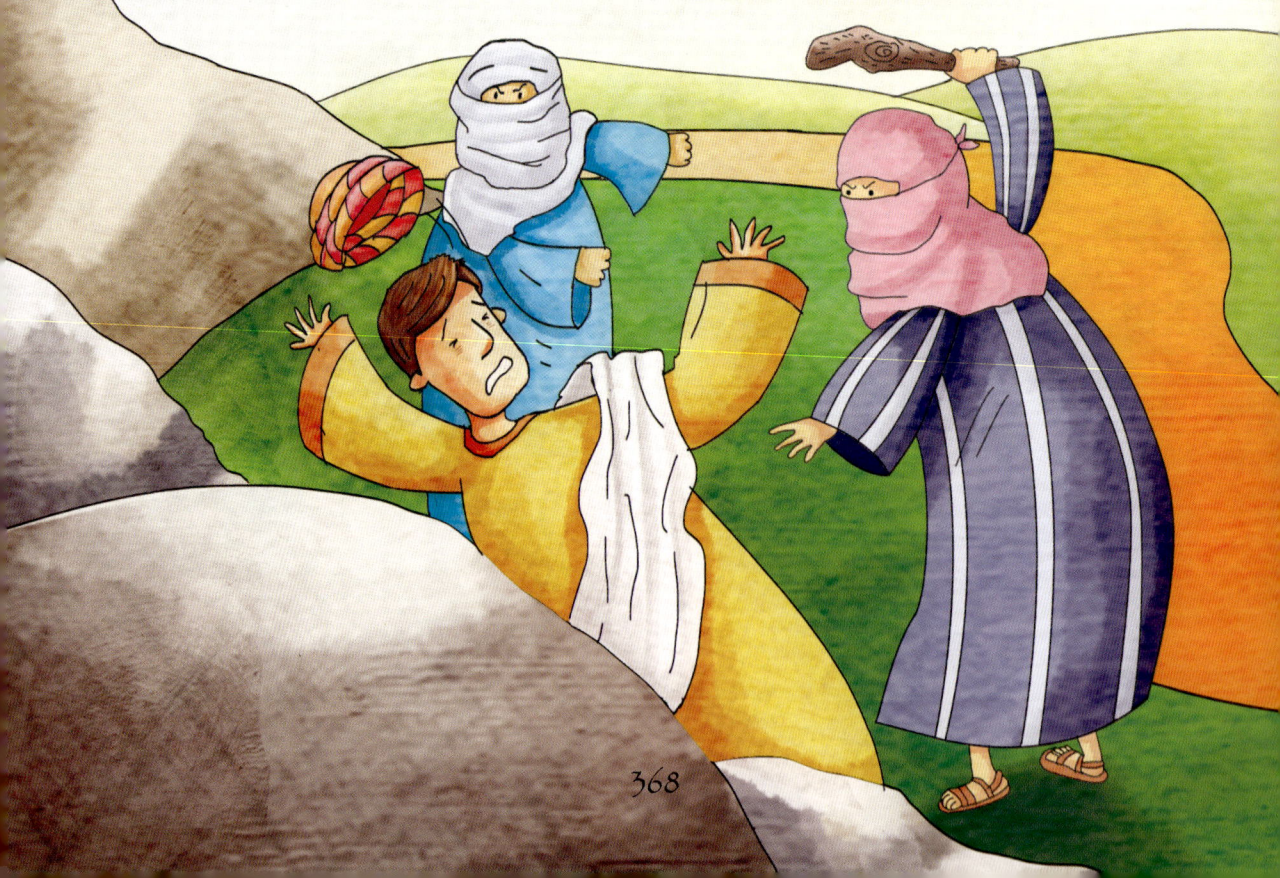

"The poor man lay bleeding by the side of the road, barely able to lift his head. After a while, a priest came by. Now, the priest saw the beaten man, but he looked away and turned his horse towards the other side of the road, as far away from him as he could get. He carried on his way without one further glance.

"Time passed, and then another man came walking along the road. This man was a Levite who worked in the temple in Jerusalem. But he, too, turned his face the other way and quickly walked by without stopping.

"Then, along the road, came a Samaritan." (Now, the Jews and the Samaritans didn't get on at all well, so no one would have expected a Samaritan to stop for a Jew.)

"But this traveller did not see his enemy by the roadside—he saw a poor injured man who needed help. He felt so sorry for him. He knelt down on the ground beside him, and carefully washed and bandaged his wounds. Then he helped him onto the back of his donkey and took him to an inn. He even gave the innkeeper money to look after the man until he was well."

Jesus looked at the man who had asked him the question in the first place. "So," he asked, "who do *you* think was a good neighbour to the injured man?"

The man sheepishly replied, "The one who was kind to him."

Jesus said, "Then go and be like him."

Being a good neighbour to someone isn't about where they live or where you live, or whether they come from the same sort of family as you or even the same country as you. It is about showing God's wonderful love to all those in need, whoever they are and wherever they may be.

The Rich Fool

Jesus wanted to warn his followers to be on their guard against all kinds of greed. Life shouldn't be about owning lots of things or making lots of money. He explained this to them in a parable:

"Once there was a rich man who owned a lot of land. One year he had a truly wonderful harvest. In fact, he had so many crops that he didn't have enough room to store them all! So he had an idea. He had plenty already, and he could have chosen to share the extra crops, but he didn't want to do that. Instead, he decided to knock down all his barns and build bigger and better ones so that he could store all his grain. That way he would have enough put aside for years, and he could spend his time enjoying himself with lots of good food and drink and generally taking life easy.

"But God said to him, 'You fool, this very night your life will be over, and who will have all this then?'"

The rich man couldn't take all his wealth with him after his death. His greed and selfishness would do him no good in the end.

Jesus was saying that we shouldn't spend our lives laying up treasure for ourselves. If God blesses us, then we should use what he gives us to help others, and then we will be rich towards God.

Be Ready!

Jesus told his followers that they needed to be ready at all times for the day when he would come again. To help them understand what he meant, he told them a story about some good servants who were waiting for their master to return from a wedding feast. They didn't know when he would be back, for in those times wedding feasts could last for days—food, wine, music, dancing—there was no knowing when he might appear at the door! Nevertheless, the faithful servants stayed dressed and ready for action, and kept the lamps cheerfully burning, so that the instant he knocked upon the door, they could open it for him.

Jesus went on to say that the servants would be richly rewarded for their readiness, for when he came back, the master be so pleased with them that he would put on an apron, sit them down at the table and wait on them himself! This is how Jesus will reward us if he returns to find us ready for him.

But things won't be so pleasant for those who are unprepared and who are sleepwalking their way through life. They are like the bad servant who loses patience while waiting for his master's return, and starts being mean to the other servants, and helps himself to food and too much drink. When the master comes back unexpectedly, he will be very angry, and the servant will surely be punished!

So let us be ready, for if we are not prepared when Jesus comes, there will be no time to get ready then. Let him instead find us watching, waiting and serving God as best we can.

The Wise and Foolish Girls

Jesus told his followers another story to help them to understand that they must be ready at all times for his return, for they would never know when it might happen.

"Once ten girls were waiting to join a wedding feast. They didn't know how long it would be before the bridegroom would turn up, and so they all brought lamps with them, but only five of the girls thought to bring some spare oil with them. The other five brought their lamps but didn't have any spare oil.

"They were excited and chattered happily amongst themselves, but time passed by and the bridegroom didn't come, and one by one, the tired girls fell asleep.

"Suddenly, at midnight, a cry rang out, for the bridegroom was coming, and the girls woke up with a start. They rushed to light their lamps, but those of the foolish girls began to flicker straight away, for their oil had run out."

"The foolish girls turned to the other girls and begged them to spare them some of their oil, but the wise girls replied sadly, 'No, there isn't enough for all of us. You'll have to go and buy some more!' And the wise girls went off to join the bridegroom and went in with him to the feast.

"By the time the foolish girls returned with lighted lamps, the door was shut, and though they knocked loudly, they were told, 'You are too late. I don't know who you are!'"

Jesus told his disciples, "Always be ready, because you don't know the day or the hour of my return!"

What must we do to be prepared? Invite Jesus to come into our hearts!

The Useless Fig Tree

Jesus once told a story about a man who had a fig tree in his vineyard. One day, the man went to look at it, hoping to find some fruit, and was disappointed to see that there was none on it. He went and found the gardener and said to him, "Look, I've been coming to check on this tree for three years now, and it hasn't produced a single fig! What's going on? I really think it's about time you cut down! It's using up precious soil for nothing."

But the gardener pleaded with his master to leave the tree for one more year to see if it would bear fruit. "Master," he said, "why don't I dig up the soil all around the tree. And I'll pop in some fertilizer too. Let's give it another year, and if it still isn't producing any fruit then I promise I will cut it down." His master agreed.

Many people believe that in this parable Jesus was referring to the nation of Israel who had lost their way. But the message is for all of us even today: God is the owner of the vineyard, and Jesus is his gardener. Jesus has come to plead for more time for us to bear fruit—and, more than that, he is prepared to help us by tending the soil around us! Let's make the most of his tender care and bear fruit for him.

The Great Banquet

"Once," said Jesus, "there was a king who was planning on holding a great feast. It was to be a very special occasion for it was to celebrate his son's wedding. The excited king spent days planning it and inviting all the people that he wanted to share the occasion with.

"At last, it was time. The table was laid, the food was ready. The king sent his servants off to tell the guests that it was time to come. You would have thought that they would have been thrilled to have been invited to such a nice meal, but every last one of them had some or other excuse—they were busy with work, they had to feed the animals, their wife was sick, and so on and so forth. Not one of them bothered to stop what they were doing and come to the feast—and some of them were even rude and nasty to the servants!

"When the king heard this, he was furious. 'They don't deserve to come!' he told his servants in disgust. 'Go back outside, and this time go and invite all the poor people, anyone who is blind or crippled or lame and bring them in to enjoy the banquet!'

"And when this had been done, and there were still some empty places at the table, the king told his servants to search even farther afield and find yet more people, and make them come in so that his house would be full. As for the original, ungrateful guests who couldn't be bothered to turn up, the king vowed that not a single one of them would get even a taste of his feast!

"And what a wonderful feast it was! The tables were creaking under the weight of all the tasty dishes and delicious things to eat, and there were jugs and jugs of the very best wine. Everyone had a lovely time!"

God had invited his people to be saved through his Son, Jesus Christ, but many of them, especially the Pharisees and the teachers of the law, had refused to accept Jesus as their Saviour—they had made all kind of excuses to explain why he wasn't the Son of God, and had taken refuge in all their laws and traditions. So God extended his invitation all across the world—to everybody, not just the Jews.

God has invited us all to his wonderful feast—let's not miss out!

"I Forgive You (seventy-seven times)!"

Jesus tried to make his followers understand how important forgiveness was. Once Peter asked him, "Lord, how many times should I forgive someone who has done something bad to me? Up to seven times?"

Jesus looked him straight in the eyes. "Don't just forgive him seven times, Peter. Forgive him seventy-seven times!" he answered. This was important, so he told one of his special stories, so that those listening could think about it very carefully.

"The kingdom of heaven," said Jesus as people stopped what they were doing to listen, and made themselves comfortable, "is like the master whose servant owed him a great deal of money. Not just a little—a lot! When it came time to pay it back, the man didn't have enough money. He was really worried about what his master would do, so he came to see him trembling and nervously begged him for some more time.

"The kind master didn't give him more time—no, instead he cancelled the debt altogether! 'Go home to your family,' he said, 'and forget about the money!'

"So the servant rushed home to tell his wife the wonderful news!

"Now, this very same servant was owed a small amount of money by another one of the servants in the household. He went to find the other man and grabbed him round the neck, shouting, 'Give me the money you owe me!'

"When the man admitted that he didn't have enough money to pay him back right then, the first servant was furious with him. So furious, in fact, that he didn't offer him any more time to find the money, but instead made sure that he was thrown into prison then and there!

"It wasn't long before the master of the household found out what had been going on. He called the first servant in to see him. 'What have you done?' the master asked in disgust. 'I cancelled your debt because you begged me to. You should have shown the same kindness to this other man as I showed to you—but no, you have been cruel and unkind, and I am really disappointed in you!' The master was so angry that he handed the servant over to the jailers until he could pay back all he owed."

Jesus looked at his followers. "This is how my Father will treat you unless you forgive your brother or sister from your heart."

Just as God forgives us over and over again, Jesus taught us that we need to forgive those around us—over and over again.

Lost and Found

The Pharisees and the teachers of the law got rather upset when Jesus hung out with the wrong sort of people. They muttered amongst themselves when they saw Jesus mixing with tax collectors and with people who had done bad things. They didn't really seem to understand what Jesus was trying to say about forgiveness. He tried to get them to see that there will be far more rejoicing in heaven over the one sinner who repents than over the ninety-nine good people who don't need to repent.

He said to them, "Imagine you had a hundred sheep and lost one of them. How would you feel? Wouldn't you leave the other ninety-nine safe and sound, and rush off to look for the lost one? Don't you think you would search high and low, in the wind or the rain or the snow, and keep on searching until you found it? And when you did find it, don't you think you would be so thrilled that you would rush home and celebrate?"

"Or picture a woman," continued Jesus, "who had ten silver coins and who lost one of those precious coins. Wouldn't she light a lamp? Don't you think she would take a brush and sweep every single corner of the room, and search every nook and cranny until she found it? And when she did find it, how happy and relieved would she be? Don't you think she would get all her friends and neighbours together and tell them about the lost coin, and how she had found it, and ask them to be happy for her?"

God cares about each and every one of us. He loves all the people who believe in him and try to live in the way he teaches. But that isn't enough. No, we are all so important to him that he will try to save every last one of us.

The Lost Son

Jesus told another story to explain how God loves to forgive us and how happy God is when sinners admit that they are wrong and return to him.

"Once there was a man who had two sons," began Jesus. "One day, the youngest son came to his father and asked him if he could have the money that he would inherit after his father died. He wanted the money now because he longed to go travelling and exploring and do lots of fun things and be his own boss. He didn't want to stay at home on the farm. It was too boring!

"The father was sad, but he gave his son the money without any argument, and sent him on his way with a sigh.

"At first, the young man had a marvellous time. He went to some wonderful places, met some interesting people and basically did whatever he wanted, whenever he wanted. He had plenty of money, so he could buy anything that took his fancy. Life was fun!"

Jesus' listeners looked at one another. Things seemed to be working out fine for the young man—what was the problem? He had everything he wanted, didn't he?

But Jesus hadn't finished. That wasn't the end of the story . . .

"Time went on," continued Jesus, "and the young man spent more and more of his money enjoying himself. Soon, all the money was gone. Every last penny! Now things weren't so much fun! The young man had no choice but to look for work, for he had no money for a place to stay or even for food. Finally, he ended up working for a pig farmer. All day long he looked after the pigs, cleaning out the mucky pigsty, and giving them food. He was so hungry that he found himself looking at the scraps he was giving to the animals and wishing he could eat it himself!

"At last he thought, 'This is ridiculous! My father feeds his servants better than this!' and he decided to go home and tell him how sorry he was and how silly he had been. 'I'm not worthy of being his son,' he thought to himself, 'but maybe he will let me work on the farm.'

"When his father saw him coming along the road, he rushed out and threw his arms around him. The young man tried to tell him that he was not fit to be called his son, but his father shushed him and told him not to speak nonsense. Then he called his servants to him and told them to bring his finest robe for his son to wear and to kill the prize calf for a wonderful feast.

"Not everyone was quite so thrilled. In fact, the older son was furious! He felt that he had worked hard for his father all this time, and nobody had ever held a feast for him! Yet now, here came his brother waltzing in, having squandered all his money, and his father couldn't wait to kill the fattened calf and welcome him home!

"'My son,' the father said to him patiently, 'you are always with me, and all I have is yours. But celebrate with me now, for your brother was dead to me and is alive again; he was lost and is found!'"

Like the boy in the story, we don't always make the right choices. Sometimes we make mistakes and do silly things. But isn't it good to know that God is always ready and willing to forgive us and to welcome us home with open arms?

The Rich Man and the Beggar

Once Jesus told a story about two very different men who led very different lives. "There was once a rich man," began Jesus, "who lived a life of luxury. He lived in a grand house, and wore fine clothes, and had lots of servants. Every day his dining table was covered from end to end with delicious plates of food. Every day was a feast!

"Now, just outside the gates to his house you would find a poor, hungry beggar named Lazarus, whose skin was covered with sores. He sat on the roadside day after day, hoping desperately for a scrap of food or a coin from whoever walked by. Lazarus had nowhere to live, and he had hardly anything to eat. As he sat outside the rich man's house, the enticing smells of the rich man's food would waft past his nose to torment him as his empty stomach rumbled with hunger. How he longed for even the crumbs which fell from the rich man's table! How happy he would have been with just their leftovers. But the rich man was selfish, and never stopped to think about poor Lazarus. In fact, he'd been sitting outside his gate for so long that he hardly even noticed him anymore.

"At last Lazarus' suffering was over, for he died and the angels carried him up to heaven to Abraham, where he felt no more pain or cold or hunger.

"Some time after, the rich man also died, but when he passed away no angels came for him. Instead, he was sent to the place for wicked people, for he had been mean and selfish. In torment, he looked up to heaven and begged, 'Father Abraham, please take pity on me and send Lazarus to dip his finger in water and cool my tongue, for I'm so thirsty!'

"But Abraham replied, 'Did you take pity on Lazarus? Did you give him food when he was hungry? You had a great time on earth, while Lazarus was suffering, but now he is looked after up here, and it is your turn to suffer.'

"'Then please, Father Abraham,' pleaded the rich man, 'at least warn my brothers before it is too late, so that they don't make the same mistakes that I did!'

"'Oh, son,' said Abraham, shaking his head sadly, 'they already have the writings of Moses and the prophets to warn them. It's their own fault if they don't change their ways in time to avoid the same fate as you!'"

Things don't always work out for us in life, but if we let God into our hearts and into our lives, he will make things right for us in heaven. And if we are given gifts in this lifetime, let's use them unselfishly to help other people who aren't as well off as we are.

The Grateful Leper

In the time of Jesus, some people suffered from horrible skin conditions. They were known as lepers, and they weren't welcome in the towns and villages, not only because they looked horrible and were rather smelly, but also because people thought that the disease might be catching. So lepers usually lived outside of the villages and stayed out of everyone's way as much as possible.

But one time when Jesus was going into a village, he was met by a sad sight—ten men, all suffering from leprosy. They stayed well back, but they cried out in loud voices, "Jesus, please take pity on us!"

Jesus felt sorry for them. He told them to go straight to the priests, and as they went, a miracle happened—they saw that their sores had completely disappeared. Their skin was smooth once again!

The excited men shouted and danced and leapt about in joy, and made their way to the priests as quickly as they could.

But one of the men, as soon as he realised that he was healed rushed straight back to Jesus, praising God at the top of his voice. He threw himself to the ground before Jesus, and thanked him with all his heart.

Jesus looked down at the grateful man. "Didn't I clean ten men? Where are the other nine? Are you the only one to come back to thank God?"

Then he said kindly, "Go on your way now. Your faith has made you well."

It is easy to get carried away with excitement when something really good happens, but let us always remember to thank God for all the wonderful things he gives us and for his everlasting love.

The Humble and the Proud

One day, Jesus looked at the crowd around him. There were many different kinds of people there—some were farmers or fishermen, others were craftsmen or market traders, but others among them thought themselves rather more educated, rather more important. Indeed, some among them thought very well of themselves, and so Jesus told a story about two men who went into a temple to pray. One of these men was a Pharisee, and the other was a tax collector.

Now, the Pharisees had very strong opinions about religion (in fact, some cared more about their religion than God!) They liked to think that they kept all of God's rules—every last one of them—and they felt that this made them rather special. They usually thought that they knew best! As for tax collectors, well, most people hated them because they got rich by taking money from other people and by giving it to the Romans (and people didn't like the Romans much either), and lots of tax collectors cheated and stole as well.

In the temple, the Pharisee stood by himself and prayed: "God, I thank you that I'm not like other people—robbers, criminals, adulterers—or even like this tax collector. I fast twice a week and give a tenth of all I get!" To be honest, it wasn't so much a prayer as bragging. The Pharisee thought he was very good and holy, and far better than everyone else!

But the tax collector stood humbly at a distance. He would not even look up to heaven, but beat his breast and said, "God, have mercy on me, for I'm nothing but a miserable sinner."

Jesus looked around at those who were listening. "It wasn't the self-important Pharisee who earned God's love and forgiveness that day—it was the humble tax collector. For all those who show off and think themselves important will be humbled, and those who humble themselves will become important."

It doesn't matter how many good things we have done, we can never be as good as Jesus, so we really don't have anything to brag about. God wants us to be humble and to think about his goodness and not about ourselves.

Bags of Gold

Jesus told his followers a story about a man who was heading off on a long journey. Before he went, this man called his three servants to him because he wanted to leave all his money with them while he went so that they could make use of it, and he gave each of them a certain number of bags depending on their abilities. He gave one of them five bags of gold, another two bags, and one bag to the third.

Some time later he returned and called the servants before him to see what they had been up to. Imagine how delighted he was when the first servant said to him,

"Sir, I put your money to work, and with the five bags of gold you gave me I have made five more." The man was very pleased and told him that since he had been able to trust him with a few things, he would gladly put him in charge of many things.

Then the second servant told him that he had gained two more bags on top of the ones that had been given to him, and again, the master was pleased that he could be trusted and put him in charge of many things.

Last of all, the third servant spoke up. "Master," he said, "I know that you are a hard man, and I was scared, so I hid the gold in a hole in the ground so it would be safe. Here it is now," and he handed over the bag of gold.

The master was angry. "You have been wicked and lazy," he exclaimed. "You could at least have put my money in the bank so it could earn some interest!" And he gave the bag of gold to the one who had ten bags, then had the worthless servant thrown out of the house!

God expects us to use whatever gifts he has given to us. If we do, he will give us even more, but if we don't, he may take them away and give them to someone who *will* use them!

The Last Will Be First

Jesus told a parable: "The kingdom of heaven is like the vineyard owner who had lots of work that needed to be done in his vineyard, so he went out early one morning to the market place to see if he could hire some workers. There were plenty of men hanging around there hoping for work, so the vineyard owner offered them a certain amount of money for the day and set them to work.

"Later on that same day, he went back to the marketplace, hired more men, and told them he'd pay them whatever was right. He did the same thing at lunchtime and in the afternoon. When he went back to the market place at about five o'clock in the afternoon, there were still some men hanging around, and he asked them what they were doing wasting their time lounging about. 'No one offered us any work,' the men said (which was a bit of a silly thing to say, since the owner had already been to the market place several times that day looking for people to hire!). The owner told them that they could come and work for him in his vineyard.

"The vineyard bustled with activity, and lots of work was done that day. When evening came, the owner called his foreman to him and told him to pay the workers, beginning with the last ones hired.

"The workers who were hired late received the same amount that had been promised to the first workers. So when those at the back of the queue, the ones who had been hired first, came to receive their pay, they expected to get more because they had worked longer, but they were given exactly the same amount as the others.

"At this, they began to grumble. 'They only worked for one hour,' complained one, 'but you've given them the same as those of us who worked all day long in the blazing heat! How is that fair?'

"The owner answered, 'I'm not being unfair. Didn't you agree to work for this amount? I paid you what we agreed. I want to give the one hired last the same as you. Don't I have the right to do what I want with my own money? Or are you annoyed because I'm being generous?'

"So the last will be first, and the first will be last."

Some people will serve God all their life, and their reward will be everlasting life in heaven. Then there are those who do bad things and don't listen to God—until the very end of their life, when they feel truly sorry for the things they have done and let God into their heart. God will reward them with everlasting life in heaven too! Everyone who believes in God and opens their heart to him will receive the same reward—not because God is being unfair to those who have believed in him all along, but because he is being generous to all of us!

The Wicked Tenants

Jesus knew that the priests and the Pharisees and the leaders were trying to catch him out all the time. They would hang around when he was talking, but they weren't really listening to what he had to say. They had hardened their hearts to his message and would not believe that he was the Son of God.

Jesus knew that the priests and the Pharisees often obeyed the letter of the law but didn't understand the real meaning of the law—they said the right things, without really letting God into their hearts and without accepting Jesus.

He told them a story. "There was once a man who had two sons. He went to the older one and said, 'Son, go and work in the vineyard today.'

"'I don't want to,' grumbled the son, but later he changed his mind and went.

"The father went to his other son and asked him the same thing.

"'Sure,' answered the son straight away, but he didn't actually go."

Jesus looked around, "Which son actually did what his father wanted?"

"The older one," they answered.

You see, what we *do* is more important than what we *say* we will do!

Jesus told another story . . .

"There was once a man who planted some grapes, rented the vineyard to some farmers and then went away. At harvest time he sent a servant to collect his share of the fruit. But instead of giving him what they owed him, the wicked tenants beat the servant and sent him away with nothing!

"The man found it hard to believe what had happened, so he sent another servant, but again they beat him and sent him away empty-handed. He sent a third, and that one was killed!

"In the end, the owner decided to send his own beloved son. 'Surely they will respect him,' he said to himself.

"But when the tenants saw him coming, they plotted amongst themselves. 'This is the owner's son,' they said. 'If we get rid of him then we will become the new owners!' And they threw him out of the vineyard and killed him."

Jesus looked at the priests and Pharisees who were listening. "What do you think the owner of the vineyard will do to the tenants when he finds out?"

"He will kill them and give the vineyard to others who will treat him fairly and give him his share," they replied. But when they realised that Jesus had really been talking about them, they felt tricked and angry!

You see, God sent many special people, such as Moses and David and Isaiah, to tell people how much he loved them, and to warn them to mend their ways. But the people didn't want to listen, and so, at last, he sent his own Son, Jesus . . .

God has given us so many chances. Let's not miss this one.

Jesus and the Children

Jesus loved little children, for they are good and innocent. He was always surrounded by children, and sometimes his disciples tried to shoo them away. They thought he had far more important things to do than be bothered by pesky little kids!

But Jesus had other ideas. "Don't ever stop little children from coming to me," he told them sternly. "The kingdom of heaven belongs to them and all those who are like them."

The disciples still didn't understand. They began arguing about which of them was Jesus' most important helper.

"I do the most!" said one.

"No, I do!" said another.

"Well, I'm definitely the cleverest!" came another voice.

"Well, I look after the money, so where would you all be without me?" claimed a fourth.

Jesus looked at them in despair and sighed. They were missing the point. God didn't care about who was the cleverest or the most powerful or the best at cooking or the best at anything at all, in fact. We don't need to do anything special to earn God's love except allow him into our lives and into our hearts. And the disciples shouldn't have been thinking about themselves so much anyway.

Jesus told them, "If you want to be first, you must be last, and you must be the servant of all." If we want to be great in God's sight, then we need to put others first and ourselves last—we should try to be a servant rather than expect other people to look after us!

Jesus beckoned one of the little children to come to him and put his arm around him.

"You see," he said, turning to the disciples, "whoever welcomes this child in my name welcomes me, and whoever welcomes me welcomes the one who sent me. For it is the one who is least among you who is the greatest. To enter heaven, you must be like a little child!"

Zacchaeus Up a Tree

Zacchaeus lived in Jericho, and there are two things that you should know about him—he was rich, and he was rather on the short side. Zacchaeus was rich because he was a tax collector, and nobody liked tax collectors, but they especially didn't like the rich ones because it was patently obvious how they had become rich—by cheating and stealing some of the precious taxes and lining their own pockets. So Zacchaeus wasn't very popular in Jericho.

Now, on this particular day, the streets of Jericho were lined with people eager to catch a glimpse of Jesus. They had all heard about this amazing man who could make people well again and perform all sorts of other miracles and tell wonderful stories, so everyone who could spare the time had crowded onto the streets to see if they could catch a glimpse of him or hear him speak.

But you need to remember the second thing about Zacchaeus—he was very short! And that was a particular problem today. No matter where he went, he couldn't see over the heads of the people in front—every last one was taller than him. Even some of the children were taller! And when he tried to squeeze his way through, they all glared at him. Nobody wanted to make room for a cheating tax collector!

Zacchaeus hopped about in frustration. He could hear the buzz of the crowd getting louder, so he knew that Jesus was nearby. He was going to miss everything!

Then he had a great idea. At the side of the road stood a nice tall, sturdy sycamore tree. No sooner had he had the thought than he shimmied up the tree trunk and perched himself precariously on an overhanging branch. He did feel rather wobbly up there—and he got some very strange looks, especially from the birds—but he didn't care! He could see everything that was happening from up there.

Zacchaeus watched excitedly as Jesus walked slowly down the street. He was going to pass right under the tree! Then he realised that Jesus wasn't going to pass right under the tree after all—no, he was going to stop there!

Zacchaeus almost fell off the branch when Jesus stopped right below, and said, "Zacchaeus, come down now. I must stay at your house today."

Zacchaeus couldn't believe his ears. Jesus knew his name! And he wanted to stay at his house! He scrambled down as fast as he could and bowed low before Jesus. All around him the crowd muttered angrily—Jesus was going to visit a sinner yet again!

Zacchaeus could hear their grumbling, but he was already a changed man. He said to Jesus, "Lord! I'm going to give half of everything I have to the poor, and if I have cheated anybody out of anything, I'll pay back four times the amount!"

Then Jesus turned to the crowd and said, "It is lost people like Zacchaeus that I came to save. Today he has found salvation!"

Jesus knows your name too, and he will never give up on you!

Martha and Mary

There were two sisters who lived in a little house in a village called Bethany. Their names were Martha and Mary. One day, Jesus and his disciples were passing through the village, and they stopped to visit!

Martha and Mary were thrilled. But they went about things rather differently. Martha rushed to sweep the floor and tidy the chairs and lay the table and prepare the food . . . and Mary just sat on the floor by Jesus' feet, not wanting to miss a single word he said.

At last, Martha could stand it no longer! "Lord," she said to Jesus, "won't you tell Mary to help me? There is so much to get ready, and she is sitting there doing nothing while I do all the work!"

"Martha, Martha," said Jesus in a soothing voice, "you are worrying about all these small things, but, do you know, they're not really what is important? Your sister understands what is truly important, and it won't be taken away from her."

Of course Jesus wasn't saying that we should laze around doing nothing and leaving the work to others. But there are times when we need to stop rushing around and look at the big picture. If Jesus came to your house to stay, would you spend your time preparing a wonderful feast with lots of fancy dishes—or would you rather spend your time with Jesus himself, listening to him and loving him?

Always remember that Jesus is the most important thing in our lives—and don't get so busy with other things that you forget to spend time with Jesus.

Lazarus Lives!

One sad day, Jesus received a message from Martha and Mary, telling him that their brother, Lazarus, was dreadfully ill. Jesus was very fond of the sisters and their brother, but he did not leave where he was for two whole days.

"Why are you still here?" asked the disciples, for they expected him to rush back to the village.

Jesus told them, "This has happened in order to bring glory to God and to the Son of God."

By the time that Jesus arrived at the sisters' village some days later, Lazarus was dead.

Martha came to meet Jesus on the road, weeping bitterly. She had loved her brother so much! "Oh, Lord," she cried, "if you had been here, my brother would not have died. But I know that even now God will give you whatever you ask."

Then Jesus said gently, "He will rise again. Everyone who believes in me will live again, even though he has died. Everyone who lives and believes in me will never really die. Martha, do you believe this?"

And Martha answered quietly, "Yes, Lord. I do believe that you are the Son of God."

Martha went back home and told Mary that Jesus was here, and Mary went to meet him, and her relatives went with her. When Jesus saw Mary weeping, and all the other relatives, then he wept too. He felt so sorry for their grief.

He asked to be taken to the cave where Lazarus had been laid, and he told the men to open it.

Now, Lazarus had been dead for four long days, but the men did as Jesus had asked them without question. When the cave was open, Jesus stood at the entrance and prayed and gave thanks to God. Then he said loudly, "Lazarus, come out!"

Everyone watched in silent wonder as a figure slowly emerged from the dark cave, his hands and feet wrapped with strips of linen and a cloth around his face. It was Lazarus, and he was alive! His sisters rushed to help him. The tears rolling down their cheeks were now tears of joy—their beloved brother had been given back to them!

For Jesus, nothing is impossible!

The Expensive Perfume

It was some time later, on an evening shortly before Passover. Jesus was having dinner with his disciples and friends in Bethany. Mary came up to him, carrying a large jar of expensive perfume. Kneeling before him, she carefully poured the perfume on his feet, using her own hair to wipe them. The whole house was filled with the wonderful fragrance.

But not everyone was pleased. One of the disciples, Judas Iscariot, was angry. "What a waste!" he complained. "That perfume was worth a year's wages. We could have sold it and given the money to the

poor!" (That all sounded very well meaning, but the truth was that Judas Iscariot didn't really care that much about the poor. In fact, he was a thief. His job was to look after the money for Jesus and the disciples, and he used to help himself whenever he felt like it!)

Jesus hushed him. "Judas," he said gently, "what Mary did was lovely. You will always have the poor, and you can help them any time you want. But you won't always have me. People will remember Mary's kindness to me."

For Jesus would not be with them in this way for much longer. The final stage of his time on earth was about to begin.

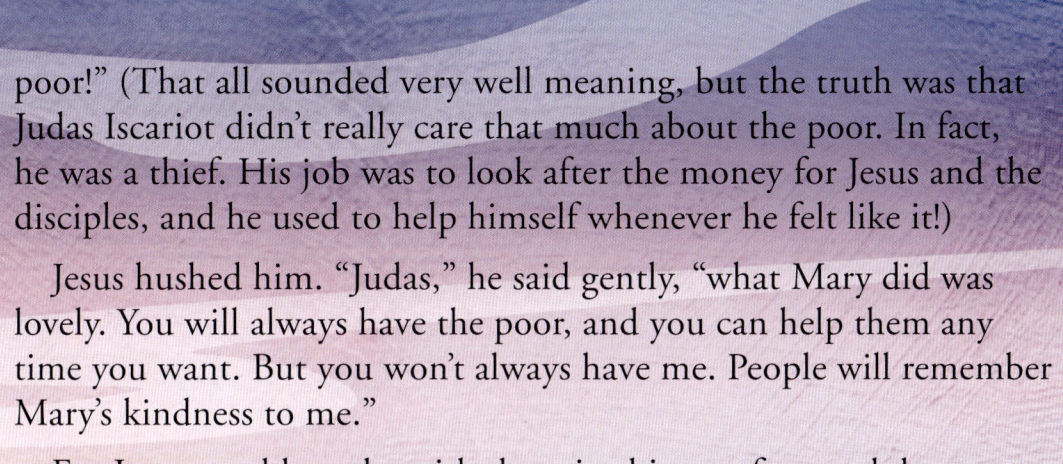

Jesus Enters Jerusalem

It was a springtime Sunday in Jerusalem, and the city was packed to bursting. It was a special time, for it was the week of the Passover festival, and everyone had gathered to celebrate.

There was something else to celebrate too, for Jesus had come to Jerusalem. People had heard about the miracles he had performed, and while the religious leaders weren't too keen on him, many of the people saw Jesus as their true King, and they tried to give him a king's welcome.

He probably didn't look much like a king though. Where was the chariot? The trumpets? The servants? No, when Jesus entered Jerusalem he was riding a young colt, a humble donkey that his followers had fetched from a nearby village.

But that didn't stop the excitement. Some of the crowd threw their cloaks or large palm leaves on the dusty ground before him. Others waved the palm leaves high in the air, and they cried out, "Hosanna to the Son of David! Blessed is the king who comes in the name of the Lord—the King of Israel!"

Many of these people hoped that Jesus would be their king—a leader who would free them from the Romans. They didn't understand that his kingdom wasn't in this world but in heaven—Jesus came to earth to die for our sins so that we could join him in his heavenly kingdom—and soon their elation would turn to bitterness and disappointment, when he did not do what they wanted him to do.

But for now, they were excited, and were making quite a stir. Some of the religious leaders didn't like it, and they told Jesus to stop his followers from making so much noise. Jesus looked at them, "If they remain silent," he said, "then the stones themselves would cry out!"

Jesus knew his mission on earth was almost finished. And he knew that in a short time these people cheering would turn against him.

Before coming to Jerusalem, he had told his friends that when he came to the city all the things that the prophets had spoken about would come true. The Son of Man would be condemned to death. He would be mocked and hurt and crucified, but three days later he would be raised to life. Right now, the disciples didn't understand the truth. But Jesus knew exactly what was going to happen to him, and he never, ever thought about not going through with it. For he knew it was God's will, and that it was the only way to save those he loved for all time.

Troublemaker

As far as the priests and Pharisees and the Jewish elders were concerned, Jesus was causing trouble in Jerusalem. The very first thing he did when he came into the city was to visit the temple and throw out all the greedy, cheating money lenders and market traders

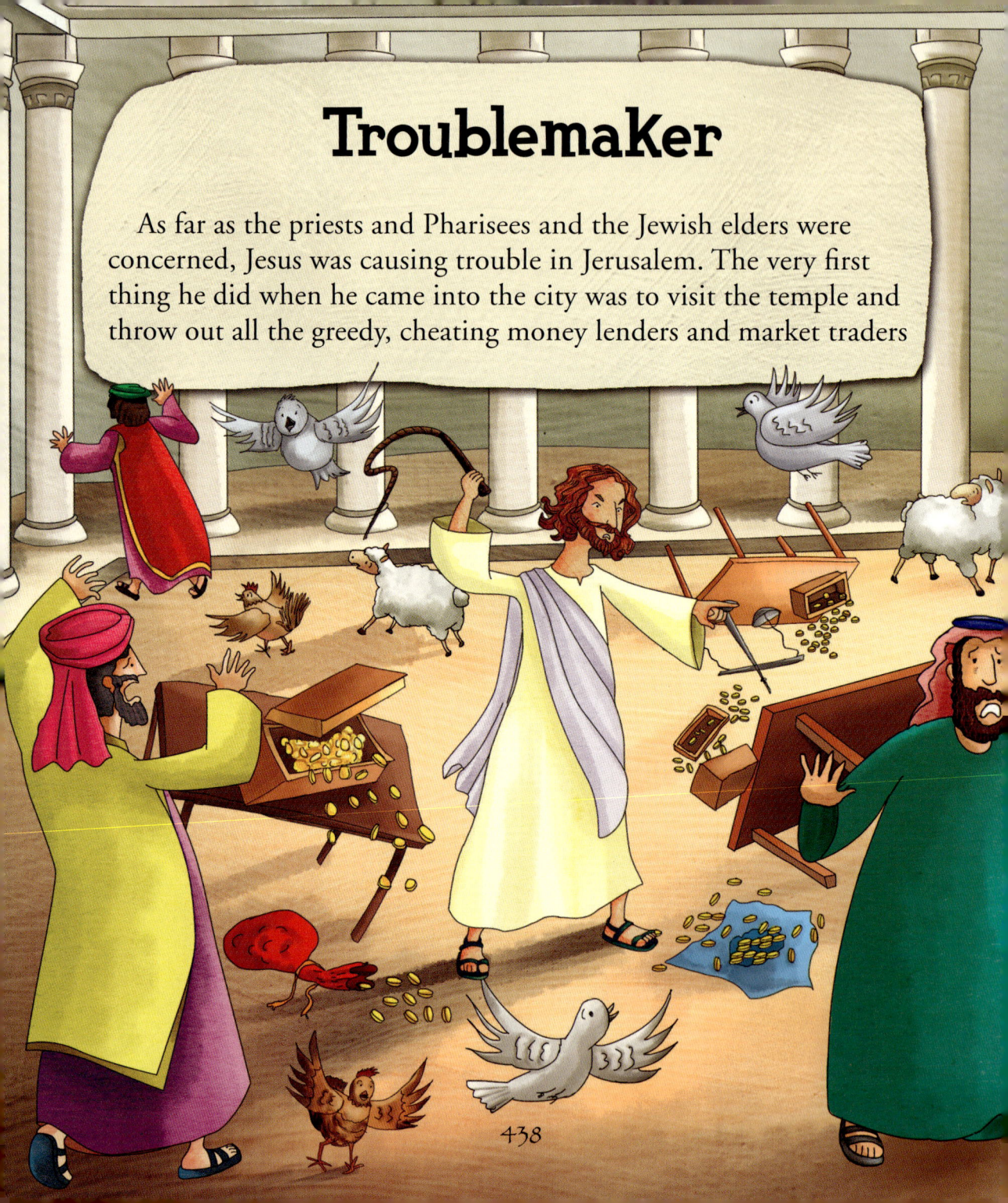

who had set up shop there to make money out of the poor people who came to make sacrifices to God. Jesus' fans might think that the temple was a far nicer place now, perfect for prayer and teaching, but as far as the priests were concerned, Jesus had no right to do what he had done (and they had made their fair share of money out of those money lenders and market traders too!). They particularly hated the fact that people were flocking to the new, improved temple to listen to Jesus and to come to him for healing, rather than to them.

No, Jesus was a rebel and a trouble maker and a pain in the neck, and he had to go! And if they didn't get onto it themselves, and he stirred up a real rebellion, then they were worried that Rome would turn its beady eye on Jerusalem, and who knew what would happen then! Especially at Passover, for after all, Passover celebrated the time when God brought the Israelites out of slavery in Egypt into the Holy Land, so it was a bit of a touchy issue with the Romans.

For the priests and Pharisees and elders, the only problem with getting rid of Jesus (apart from the small fact that technically he hadn't done anything illegal!) was that the people in the city loved him so much, and they didn't want to make them angry, especially during the festival. So they went about trying to catch him out, sending spies to follow him and trap him into saying something that they could arrest him for then and there. But Jesus saw through all their tricks and refused to play their game.

In the end, they decided to just arrest him anyway, but that wasn't so easy, for he always seemed to be surrounded by his followers. They needed some help—and that help came from one of Jesus' own disciples!

Judas Iscariot was dishonest. He looked after the money for Jesus and the rest of the disciples, and he kept some back for himself instead of giving it to those who needed it. In the end, his greed made him do a very bad thing. Judas went to the chief priests in secret and asked them how much they would give him if he delivered Jesus into their hands.

The priests couldn't believe their ears! They knew that Judas was one of Jesus' closest, most trusted friends. They offered him thirty silver coins, the going price for a common slave . . . and Judas accepted! As soon as he had left the temple, the priests rubbed their hands in glee. They couldn't believe it had been so easy! Now they had someone else to do their dirty work for them.

From then on, Judas was simply waiting for the opportunity to hand Jesus over.

Two Small Coins

Jesus was sitting in the temple, watching people put money in the collection boxes as offerings to God. Many rich people put in lots of clinking coins, making sure everybody knew how good they were being! Then along came a poor widow, her young children in threadbare clothes and bare feet. She put in two small copper coins. Together, they were worth less than a penny!

Jesus turned to his disciples. "Did you see that poor widow?" he asked. "The truth is, she gave far more than anyone else here today." The disciples looked puzzled. Surely her coins had been almost worthless!

Jesus tried to make them understand: "All those rich people had so much money that it was easy for them to give huge offerings—they still had plenty left. But that poor widow gave everything she had to give. She clearly loves God with all her heart, and trusts him to look after her, for she gave him everything she had."

Like a Servant

It was nearly time for the Passover feast, and a kind man had set aside a room in his own house for the disciples to prepare for it. That night, when they were eating, Jesus left the table, wrapped a towel around his waist, filled a basin with water and then, kneeling on the floor, began to wash and dry the disciples' feet like a servant.

The disciples were speechless. In those days people's feet got ever so dirty because they wore open sandals on dusty roads, but it would usually be the job of the very lowest servant to go about kneeling on the floor and washing the dirt away. What on earth was Jesus doing?

So when Jesus knelt before Simon Peter, the disciple threw up his hands in horror, "Lord, you mustn't wash my smelly feet! That's not your job!"

Jesus replied gently, "You don't understand what I'm doing, Peter, but soon you will. Unless you let me wash away the dirt, you won't really belong to me."

When Jesus said this, Peter begged him to wash his hands and head too! But Jesus answered, "If you have bathed then you only need to wash your feet; your body is clean."

Then Jesus washed the rest of the disciples' feet, one by one, until they were all clean.

When he finished, he said to them, "Do you understand what I was doing? You call me 'Lord' and 'Teacher,' and that is what I am—but I'm your servant too. The master isn't more important than the servant. I washed your feet, so you should wash one another's feet too."

Jesus had washed their feet like a servant, so that they could learn to do the same for one another.

Jesus was sad and troubled. He knew he would soon have to leave his friends. "Soon, one of you will betray me," he said sorrowfully. The disciples looked at one another in shock. Who could he possibly mean? They all loved him and would follow him to the ends of the earth!

Well, that was true for eleven of them. But one was about to betray Jesus—and do you know, Jesus felt sorry for him! The others had no idea what Jesus was talking about. They had no idea who the traitor was, but Jesus said softly to Judas Iscariot, "Go and do what you have to do," and Judas left. But the others still didn't understand—they probably thought he was going off to do something with the money (which I suppose he was).

Now Jesus handed around some bread, saying, "This is my body, which will be broken." Next, he passed around a cup of wine, saying, "Drink this—it is my blood, which will take away sin." He wanted them to remember this time with him, and hoped they would one day understand what he was really telling them.

Then he said that he would soon be leaving them.

At this, the disciples called out in dismay. Simon Peter cried out, "But Lord, where are you going? Why can't I follow you? I would lay down my life for you a hundred times over!"

"Would you, my friend?" asked Jesus gently. "And yet you will disown me three times before the cock crows!" Peter was horrified. He knew—he just *knew*—that he would never do such a dreadful thing.

Jesus knew how upset the disciples were at the news he had given them. He tried to comfort them.

"My dear friends," he said, "I am going ahead to prepare a place for you in my Father's house. You will know how to find your own way there."

"How?" cried the disciples in confusion.

"I am the way and the truth and the life," replied Jesus. "The only way to the Father is through believing in me. If you really know me, you will know my Father as well.

"As just as my Father has loved me, so have I loved you. And I give you this command: love one another, just as I have loved each of you, and everyone will know that you are my disciples. There is no greater love than to lay down one's life for one's friends.

"And don't lose hope if everyone seems out to get you, if the whole world seems to hate you—just remember that it hated me first. It is because you don't belong to it that it will hate you!"

Jesus wanted his disciples to never ever give up, however much the world seemed against them. And he wants you to never give up too. If people are ever mean to you because you love Jesus—well, you are in the best company of all!

Betrayed with a Kiss

That night, Jesus and the disciples left the hustle and bustle of the busy city and went to a quiet garden filled with olive trees set on a hillside. Jesus wanted to pray to his Father. He asked Peter, James and John to keep him company and to wait nearby while he went off on his own to talk to his Father.

His heart was filled with sadness, for he knew what was about to happen, and he was dreading it. In misery, he cried out, "Oh, Father, is there any other way? Does it have to happen like this?" yet his very next words were, "But let it be not as I want, but as you want."

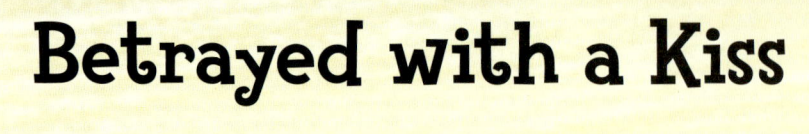

What was going to happen would be terrible beyond belief, but Jesus knew that God wasn't making him do anything—he had chosen freely to do it. He trusted in God and knew that this was the only way to save God's children. He needed to take all their sins upon himself, and he needed to take their punishment too. He would be their scapegoat, so that they could be free from their sins, and free to be close to God again. It was the plan, and Jesus believed in the plan. But he knew it was going to be so, so hard.

Sadly he returned to Peter, James and John. He felt even more alone when he found his friends fast asleep. They couldn't even stay away with him for one hour!

He spoke to his Father two more times that night, and each time the disciples couldn't keep their eyes open and dozed off. The last time, when he came back to them he awoke them to say, "The hour has come. You need to get up, for the one who betrayed me is here!"

And so he was, for at that moment a huge crowd of people burst into the quiet garden with lanterns and swords and heavy clubs. And at the head of them all was Judas Iscariot, come to earn his precious silver coins. He had told the chief priests that he would kiss Jesus so that they would know whom to arrest, and as Judas approached him, Jesus said sadly, "Oh, Judas, would you betray the Son of Man with a kiss?"

When he realised what was happening, Simon Peter was filled with anger, and he struck out with his sword, cutting off the ear of one of the crowd that had come to do the High Priest's dirty work.

"No, Peter," said Jesus, making him put away his sword, and healing the man's ear. "Don't you think my Father would send a host of angels to save me if I asked him to? This has to happen—how else can everything the prophets said about me be fulfilled?"

Then he turned to the soldiers. "I'm the one you have come to find," he said quietly. "Let these others go. You had no need to come here with swords and clubs. You could easily have taken me when I was in the temple courts."

The disciples were filled with despair. They could see clearly now that Jesus wasn't going to try to escape or fight, and as he let himself be arrested, they ran away in fear and went into hiding.

By the flickering light of their torches the guards led Jesus through the streets of Jerusalem to the house of Caiaphas, the chief priest of the Jews. He was the one who had sent them to arrest Jesus, and he was waiting for them there, along with the other high priests who made up the council. All this was very wrong. The Jewish law of the time didn't allow trials to take place at night, and definitely not in someone's house. But that didn't bother the priests—they had already decided Jesus was guilty!

Now, they needed to find a reason to order Jesus' execution, but they had a small problem—they didn't have any evidence against him. Not to worry, they thought. It was easy enough to persuade some people to come and tell lies about him. Unfortunately for them,

though, the 'witnesses' that they found couldn't seem to agree on the same story, so they were back to square one.

Caiaphas decided that the easiest thing would be to get Jesus to commit blasphemy (blasphemy is speaking about God in a disrespectful way).

"So," he said to Jesus, "tell us, are you the Son of God?"

"You have said it yourself," Jesus answered. "And I will tell you this: you will see the Son of God sitting at the right hand of the Almighty God, riding on the clouds of heaven."

"Enough!" the High Priest cried. "This man claims to be the Son of God. This is blasphemy—this man must die!"

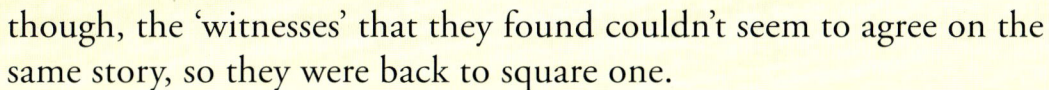

A Cock Crows

While all this was happening, Simon Peter was waiting miserably outside in the courtyard. When the soldiers had taken Jesus to be questioned, Simon Peter had followed them to the house of the high priest, and now he waited with a heavy heart and filled with fear, along with the guards warming themselves at the fire. As one of the servant girls was walking by, she caught sight of Peter by the fire. It was pretty dark in the courtyard, but there was enough torchlight to see by, and the man looked a bit familiar. She peered more closely at Peter's face. Then it dawned on her: "Weren't you with Jesus of Nazareth?" she asked. "I'm sure I saw you with him."

"No, no! You've got the wrong man!" Peter hissed quietly, hoping no one else had heard, for he was terrified about what might happen if they thought he was one of Jesus' disciples.

The girl simply shrugged and walked away, but a little while later she crossed the courtyard on her way back. She glanced at Peter again, then she said to one of the guards, "Don't you think he looks like one of Jesus' followers?"

"I told you, I don't have anything to do with him!" babbled Peter in a panic before the guard could reply.

But now everyone was looking at him. "You must be one of them," said one of the guards suspiciously. "I can tell from your accent you're from Galilee."

"I swear I've never even met him!" cried Peter, his heart racing.

At that very moment, a cock crowed, and Peter remembered what Jesus had said only a few hours ago, and he broke down and wept in dismay. How could he have betrayed Jesus like that! He felt as if his heart had broken in two.

Pilate Washes his Hands

"This man must die!" Caiaphas had said, but it wasn't as straightforward as that.

Unfortunately for the High Priest, the Jews weren't allowed to execute anyone—the Romans liked to keep that sort of thing all to themselves. And more than that, the Romans wouldn't really care much about whether or not Jesus thought he was the Son of God, because they didn't believe in God anyway.

So the priests had to come up with another plan. They decided to tell the Romans that Jesus was calling himself 'King of the Jews'. The Romans would certainly care about that! The Jews weren't allowed to have any kings—they were all subjects of the mighty Roman Emperor! If Jesus claimed to be a king, then that was treason—and in Rome, instant death was the penalty for treason!

So Jesus was taken before Pontius Pilate, the Roman governor. Now, to be honest, Pilate was out for an easy life. He asked Jesus a few questions, read a few reports, and could see perfectly well that Jesus wasn't a threat at all. Jesus about to lead a rebellion of Jews against Rome? Not a chance! The man was clearly innocent, but that wasn't what the crowd wanted to hear.

You see, by now, quite a crowd had gathered. The rumour had spread: Jesus of Nazareth was on trial for his life. Those very same people who, just a few days before, had cheered and waved as Jesus entered Jerusalem, had now been fed lies (and maybe bribes) by the priests and Pharisees and wanted blood! In fact, it was quite a mob.

Pilate saw just one way out. It was Passover, and at Passover it was the custom to release one prisoner. The crowd had a choice of two prisoners to vote for (not that they could really vote!)—Jesus of Nazareth (the one who had healed lots of people and told wonderful stories about love and forgiveness and mercy) or Barabbas (currently in prison for rebellion and murder).

Hmm . . .

Should have been a fairly obvious choice, don't you think?

But no, the crowd had been whipped into a frenzy by the priests and Pharisees and the leaders, and they all started chanting "Free Barabbas! Free Barabbas!"

"But what has Jesus done wrong?" asked Pilate.

In reply, the crowd shouted, "Crucify him! Crucify him!"

Pilate was dismayed, but he didn't want to start a riot. He didn't care enough about justice to actually do anything about it. Instead, he called for a servant to bring him a bowl of water, and he washed his hands in it. "It's your call," he was saying to the people. "I didn't have anything to do with it!"

As I said, Pilate definitely wanted an easy life. He cared more about himself than anything else.

A Shadow Falls

Soldiers led Jesus away. "So you're King of the Jews, then?" they said mockingly. "Well then, let's make sure you look the part!" and they dressed him in a purple robe, the colour worn by kings, and put a crown of sharp thorny branches upon his head. Then they beat him, and spat in his face, before putting him back in his own clothes and leading him through the streets towards Golgotha, the place where he was to be crucified.

They made him carry the wooden cross on his back, but it was large and heavy, and Jesus had been dreadfully beaten and he had had no rest all night. When he could carry the cross no longer, they snatched someone from out of the crowd to carry it for him. And so the dreadful procession made its way out of the city to the hill of Golgotha.

There on the hillside, soldiers nailed Jesus to the cross and placed above his head a sign saying, 'JESUS OF NAZARETH, KING OF THE JEWS'. As they raised the cross, Jesus cried, "Father, forgive them. They don't know what they're doing."

Two criminals were crucified beside him.

"If you're so special then why don't you save yourself? And save me too, while you're at it!" one sneered.

But the other told him to be quiet. "Look," he said to him, "we're here because we deserve to be. But Jesus hasn't done anything wrong." Then he turned to Jesus and said, "Please remember me when you come into your kingdom," and Jesus promised he would be with him that very day in Paradise.

As Jesus hung there on the cross, down below the guards drew lots to see who would win his clothes (after all, he didn't need them anymore), and the priests and Pharisees taunted him—"If you come down from the cross now, we'll believe in you!" they mocked.

Of course, Jesus could have chosen for all this to stop anytime he wanted. But he stayed there because he chose to—because he loved these people so much and wanted to save them from themselves.

At midday, a shadow passed across the sun, and dark clouds filled the sky. For three long hours darkness covered the land as though it were the middle of the night. At three o'clock in the afternoon, Jesus cried out in a loud voice, "My God, why have you forsaken me?" He had always been so close to his Father, they were one, but now he bore the sins of all the people in the world, and so he felt all alone for the first and last time.

Then he let out a great cry—"It is finished!"—and with these words, he gave up his spirit and let himself die.

At that moment the earth shook, and in the city the curtain in the holy temple was torn from top to bottom, for Jesus, through his death, had removed the barriers between God and man. There is nothing now that comes between us and God.

Back on the hill, when the Roman soldiers felt the ground move beneath their feet and saw how Jesus passed away, they were deeply shaken. "Surely he was the Son of God!" whispered one in amazement.

Though Jesus had always meant for this to happen, his friends were heartbroken at his death. They took his broken body down from the cross and carefully wrapped it, then took him to a tomb carved out of rock and laid his body inside.

But the priests and Pharisees remembered that Jesus had spoken about rising again, and so they asked Pilate to put guards on the tomb, and they had it sealed with a massive stone so that nobody could get in or out. That made sure that none of his followers could pull some sort of clever stunt with his body to try to fool people!

"That's the end of Jesus!" said the chief priests smugly.

But, of course, they were wrong . . .

The Empty Tomb

Three days later, early in the morning, before the sun had fully risen, Mary Magdalene and some other women went to anoint the body of their beloved teacher. As they walked sadly along the dusty path, they wondered amongst themselves whom they could persuade to open the tomb for them, for the stone was far too big and heavy for them to move it themselves.

But just as they came near to the tomb, the earth shook beneath their feet, the guards were thrown to the ground, and the women saw that the stone had been rolled away from the entrance. And inside the tomb, shining brighter than the sun, was an angel!

The terrified women fell to their knees, hands over their eyes, for the angel was too bright to look at (and they were too scared anyway!) But the angel said to them, "Why are you looking here for someone who is alive? This is a place for dead people! Jesus isn't here—he has risen! Don't you remember that he told you this would happen? Have a quick look, then run and tell his disciples that he will meet them in Galilee just as he promised."

So the women hurried away in excitement to tell the disciples the news, afraid yet filled with joy.

Later on that same day, Mary Magdalene stood weeping quietly outside the tomb. Peter and one of the other disciples had come, had seen the strips of linen and had gone away again, not knowing what to think, whether to be happy or sad. Now Mary was here by herself. The angel's words had filled her with hope, yet she felt so alone. All she wanted was to see Jesus one more time.

Just then she heard the sound of footsteps behind her. A man asked gently, "Why are you crying? Who are you looking for?"

This must be the gardener, she thought. Surely he would know where the body was. And she begged forlornly, "Sir, if you have moved him, please tell me where he is, and I'll get him."

The man only spoke her name, "Mary," but instantly she spun around. She recognised that clear, gentle voice!

"Teacher!" she gasped. Surely this was a dream! Was he really, truly there? And she reached out towards Jesus with her arms wide open.

Jesus said, "Dear Mary, you mustn't hold on to me, for I have not yet gone to my Father. Quick! Go and tell the others!" So Mary rushed off with the amazing news that she had seen Jesus alive! The disciples were never going to believe her!

Alive!

That same evening the disciples, all except Thomas, were huddled around a table in a dark room talking about the incredible events of the day. They had closed the shutters and locked the door because they were scared that the Jewish leaders would try to arrest them, but their thoughts were all on Jesus. Could he really be alive? They shook their heads in disbelief. Maybe the women had imagined it all.

Suddenly Jesus was with them in the room! The men started in shock. Some of them glanced at the door—no, it was still locked! He hadn't come in that way! So what was this, a ghost? And some of them were scared.

"Friends, friends," said Jesus soothingly, "why do you look so worried? Don't you believe your own eyes? It really is me."

Some of the men still looked uncertain. "Look," said Jesus, "look at my hands and feet. Here are the scars from the nails. See for yourselves!" Then he asked, "Is there any food around here?" and as the disciples watched him eat, he looked at them and laughed. "Do you still think I'm a ghost? Would a ghost be eating dinner here with you?"

And then all the disciples laughed too, and they crowded round Jesus, hugging and kissing him, with tears of joy running down their faces. They felt as if their hearts would burst with happiness.

But Thomas, as we said, wasn't there. Can you imagine how he felt when his friends told him what had happened? He just couldn't believe it. He just couldn't. "Unless I see the holes with my own eyes, and put my finger where the nails were, I won't believe," he said angrily. Because, of course, he did want to believe.

Just one week later, the disciples were all together again, Thomas too, when suddenly Jesus was amongst them again. The first thing he did was turn to Thomas. "Well, Thomas, do you believe now?" he asked. "Come nearer, look for yourself, touch the wounds with your own hands. Stop doubting, Thomas—and believe!"

Thomas fell to his knees, overcome with joy. "Oh, Lord, I do believe!" he cried out, bursting with happiness.

Jesus smiled at him, "Thomas, you believed only because you saw me yourself, with your very own eyes. Think about the people who believe without even seeing. How blessed will they be!"

Lord, help us to believe, even if we can't see you with our own eyes!

The Ascension

Jesus and his friends were on a hillside outside Jerusalem. It was time for him to leave the world. The disciples were sad that Jesus was leaving, but in the days and weeks since his resurrection, he had made many things clearer to them, and had told them a little about what the future would hold. They knew that he wasn't really leaving them—he was just going ahead to prepare the way for them. And he had promised he wouldn't be leaving them alone—he was going to send them help.

Jesus had told his disciples what to do. "You must stay here in Jerusalem for now," he had said, "and wait for the gift that my Father has promised you, for soon you will be baptised with the Holy Spirit. Then you must spread my message not only in Jerusalem and the places near here, but in every country throughout the world!"

So now, as they stood upon the hillside, the disciples were filled with hope and strength and belief. Jesus held up his hands to bless them and then, before their eyes, he was taken up to heaven, and a cloud hid him from sight.

As his friends stood looking upwards in wonder, suddenly two men dressed in white stood beside them. "Why are you looking at the sky?" they asked. "Jesus has been taken from you into heaven, but he will come back again in the same way that he left!"

Jesus has gone to heaven to prepare a place for us, and one day he will come again to take us to our new home so that we can live forever in God's love.

Flames of Fire

It was ten days since Jesus had been taken up to heaven. The disciples (or apostles) were gathered together in a room early one morning waiting for something to happen. Mind you, they didn't know what that 'something' was! All they knew was that they had lots of work to do spreading the message that Jesus had brought and the amazing news about what his death and resurrection really meant—but that Jesus himself had told them to wait here in Jerusalem until God sent them a special gift. So here they were, waiting patiently, all twelve of them … (for they had chosen a man named Matthias to join them to take the place of Judas Iscariot).

Suddenly the house was filled with the sound of a mighty rushing wind coming from heaven. The men looked around in wonder, filled with excitement, and then gasped as flames of fire seemed to rest on each person there. It was the Holy Spirit sent by God to guide and help them in their special mission, making a home inside their hearts. They couldn't see the Holy Spirit—just like the wind—but they could feel it, deep within them.

The men were all filled with the Holy Spirit, and straight away they began to speak in different languages—languages they had never spoken before or studied! Can you imagine that? All of a sudden being able to speak Greek or Mandarin or Basque or Urdu? Wouldn't that be amazing? Wouldn't it be a miracle?

Hearing the commotion, a huge crowd gathered outside. You can imagine how taken aback they were when the apostles came out of the house and began to talk to them in different languages!

"What's going on?" they exclaimed in amazement. "How are they doing this?"

There were people there from Asia and Egypt, from Libya and Crete, from Rome and Arabia—and each and every one of them was being told all about God in their very own language. And yet, all the apostles were from Galilee!

Of course, there are always some people who can't take things seriously. Some people only wanted to make fun of what was happening.

"They've all had too much wine!" they mocked. "They're drunk!"

Peter stepped forward confidently. "Listen!" he said clearly, so that everyone could hear him. "Don't be ridiculous! It's nine o'clock in the morning—of course we're not drunk! We have been filled with the Holy Spirit! Just a few weeks ago Jesus from Nazareth died on a cross. Yet ask any one of us and we can tell you that God has raised Jesus to life! We have all seen him with our very own eyes!

"You see, this was all part of God's plan. You know deep down that Jesus really was sent to you by God—think about all the miracles he performed, all the signs he showed you. Jesus was handed over to you, and you rejected him, and had him killed by evil men. But God planned it all. Jesus died, but death could not hold him! God made Jesus your Lord and Messiah!"

The people looked worried and unhappy. What had they done? And how could they ever make it better?

Peter looked at their faces. He knew what they were feeling. "If you really are sorry," he went on, "then repent. Be baptised in the name of Jesus Christ, and the bad things that you have done will all be forgiven. And just like us, you will receive the wonderful gift of the Holy Spirit! This promise is not just for you, but for your children, too, and for people who are far away—God's gift is for everyone!"

Many, many people believed in Jesus that day, and soon the word spread, and more and more people learnt the wonderful news and joined God's own family.

Getting Into Trouble... and Out Again!

Of course, not everybody was happy with the way things were going. The Jewish priests and leaders had thought they had got rid of Jesus, but now they must have been feeling as though they had stirred up a hornet's nest! Instead of one trouble maker, now they seemed to have lots—and it was getting worse all the time! Maybe if his annoying followers had just stuck with talking things would have been alright, but oh, no, not them . . .

One day, Peter and John were making their way to the temple to pray when they spotted a man begging outside the gates. Now, this poor man had been lame ever since he was born, and that made it very difficult to get a job, so he spent every day outside the temple, hoping that some kind passerby would be able to spare him a coin or two. When Peter and John stopped in front of him, he looked up hopefully.

"I'm afraid I don't have any money," said Peter, and the man's heart sank. Yet Peter hadn't finished speaking. "But," the apostle went on, "I can give you something far better!" As the lame man looked decidedly puzzled, Peter continued, "In the name of Jesus Christ, I order you to get up and walk!" And to everyone's astonishment—especially the beggar himself—Peter held out his hand and helped him to his feet. He couldn't believe what was happening—he was actually standing up on his own two feet! Flabbergasted, the man tried a few cautious steps, and then a few more, and a few more still. Then he jumped up and down a bit, and gave a little leap in the air.

"Oh, Lord!" he cried in delight and gratitude, "how truly wonderful you are!"

Then he carried right on walking straight into the temple to thank God over and over again for the amazing thing Peter had done!

The people could hardly believe that this was the same man who had sat outside the temple every day to beg. They all crowded round Peter and John.

"Hold on a minute," said Peter. "We didn't make this man walk all by ourselves. God did it. It was faith in the name of Jesus that healed this man! So praise God!"

The people were amazed. They listened to what Peter had to say, and then they all rushed off to tell their friends and neighbours.

Naturally, it wasn't long at all before the Jewish leaders heard about the miraculous healing and heard the apostles talking to the people. They were so angry that they threw them into prison, saying, "Who gave you the right to do this?" which was a bit silly really, and probably sounded sillier still when Peter calmly replied that it was by the name of Jesus Christ that the man had been healed. Anyway, the next day they had to let them go—after all, everyone had seen the lame man walk, so what could they do, apart from tell them to keep their mouths shut?

But things went from bad to worse as far as the Jewish priests and leaders were concerned. Nobody seemed to want to listen to them any more, all that anybody could talk about were the apostles and their wonderful words and healing. So they threw the apostles back in prison again (they really weren't very clever, were they?)—but do you know what happened this time? In the middle of the night they had a very special visitor—an angel! The angel opened the prison doors and led the men out and told them to go back to the temple and carry on spreading the good news.

Well, when the priests called for the apostles to be brought before them the next day, they got a very nasty surprise.

"They just disappeared!" said the terrified guards. "Honestly—the doors are still locked!"

When the apostles were finally found (at the temple, obviously), the priests accused them of disobeying their instructions. But Peter and the others bravely replied, "We must obey God rather than human beings!"

Some priests wanted to have them executed, but one said wisely, "If they are just stirring up rebellion, in the end it will all fizzle out. But if they really are from God, then you won't be able to stop them, and will find yourselves fighting against God!"

So the apostles were released under strict instructions not to talk about Jesus any more—but of course they did! And more and more people listened to them, and more and more people believed.

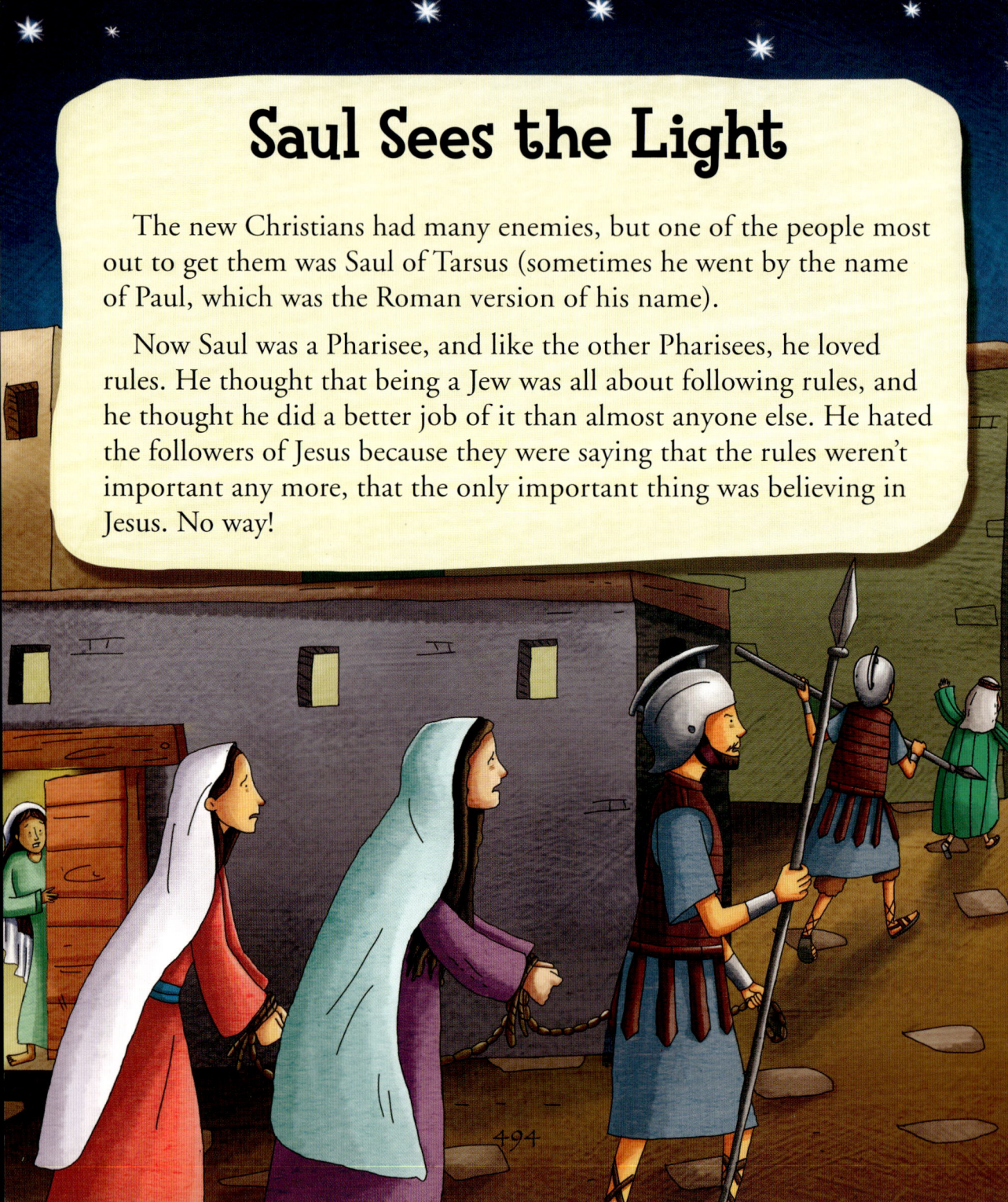

Saul Sees the Light

The new Christians had many enemies, but one of the people most out to get them was Saul of Tarsus (sometimes he went by the name of Paul, which was the Roman version of his name).

Now Saul was a Pharisee, and like the other Pharisees, he loved rules. He thought that being a Jew was all about following rules, and he thought he did a better job of it than almost anyone else. He hated the followers of Jesus because they were saying that the rules weren't important any more, that the only important thing was believing in Jesus. No way!

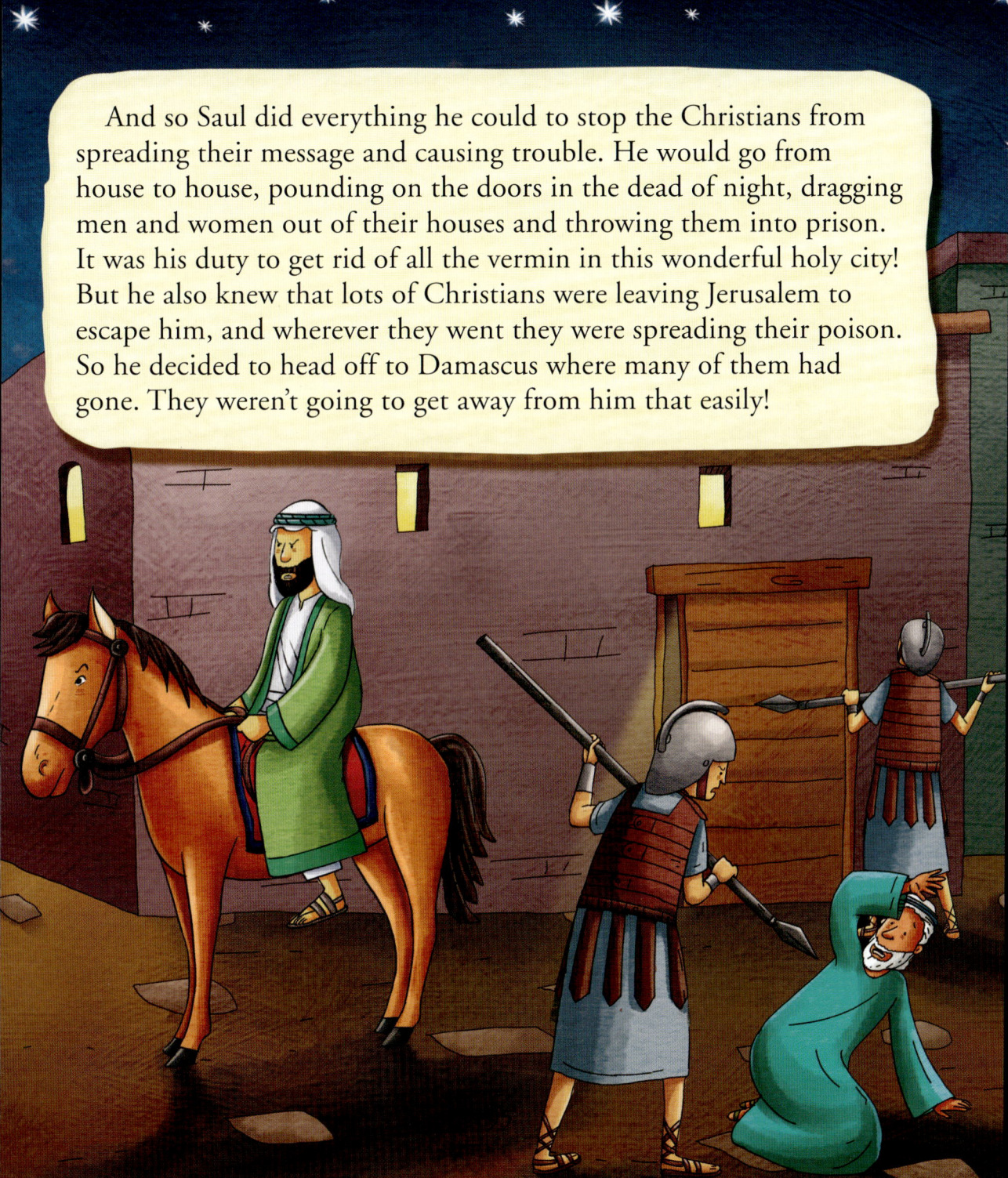

And so Saul did everything he could to stop the Christians from spreading their message and causing trouble. He would go from house to house, pounding on the doors in the dead of night, dragging men and women out of their houses and throwing them into prison. It was his duty to get rid of all the vermin in this wonderful holy city! But he also knew that lots of Christians were leaving Jerusalem to escape him, and wherever they went they were spreading their poison. So he decided to head off to Damascus where many of them had gone. They weren't going to get away from him that easily!

Saul was making his way along the dusty road to Damascus, probably thinking about all the troublesome people he was going to catch, when suddenly, a blinding light from heaven flashed down. Saul fell to the ground, covering his eyes. What was happening?

Then he heard a voice say, "Saul, why do you keep on persecuting me?"

Saul began trembling. He thought he knew who was speaking, but he had to ask.

"I am Jesus," replied the voice, just as he had known it would. "Get up and go into the city, and someone will meet you and tell you what to do."

Saul had some guards with them, and they didn't have a clue what was happening! They had heard the voice, but they didn't see any light—what was going on, and why was Saul down on the ground with his eyes tight shut?

Saul struggled shakily to his feet, but when he opened his eyes, he couldn't see a thing! His guards had to take him by the hand and lead him into the city. There he stayed for three days without eating or drinking, spending his time in prayer. He had so much to think about—everything he had believed had been wrong. He had thought that what he was doing was pleasing God—now he had found out that he had been hurting him. But there was still time to change his ways and try to undo the dreadful things he had done.

You see, God had great plans for Saul. Saul was going to be the one to spread the news far and wide—farther than anyone else—and so God sent a Christian named Ananias to the house where he was staying. When he got there, Ananias laid his hands on Saul, and it was as if scales had fallen from his eyes, and Saul could see once more! And now, filled with the Holy Spirit, he saw everything so much more clearly.

Saul (or Paul) began to spread the good news about Jesus in Damascus, and people could hardly believe their ears.

"Didn't this man used to be our enemy?" they would ask in astonishment. "Is it really the same man?" But while his enemies became his friends, his old friends soon became his enemies. In the end, it wasn't safe for him to stay in Damascus any longer, but he couldn't just walk out the front gate since the soldiers were looking for him. Do you know how he escaped? His friends hid him in a large basket and carefully lowered it over the city walls under cover of night! Once he was safely down, Saul jumped out of the basket and made his way back to Jerusalem. Now that he had met Jesus and had seen the light, he realised that all the rules he had been so hung up on before were not important. The only important thing in life was knowing Jesus.

With this truth in his heart, Saul went on to become one of the greatest of all the apostles.

The Sheet of Animals

Do you ever have strange dreams? Have you ever wondered if they were trying to tell you something? Well, one day Peter had a dream, and it was very strange indeed.

Peter was lying on a roof top by the sea. He had been praying to God, but it was hot on the roof, and he had dozed off. In his dream, he could a huge white sheet being lowered from heaven by its corners. The sheet was filled with all sorts of mammals, reptiles and birds. Looking closely, he realised that they weren't just any old animals—they were all creatures that Jews were forbidden to eat, for they were considered 'unclean.' It was one of the many things that made them different from Gentiles—people who weren't Jews. Peter was a Jew, and he had always followed the rules. He knew what he was allowed to eat and what he wasn't.

So imagine his surprise and shock when he heard God's voice saying, "Get up, Peter. Kill and eat."

"Surely not, Lord!" Peter replied in horror. "I have never eaten anything unclean in all my life!"

The voice said, "Don't call impure what God has made clean."

This happened three times, and then the sheet was pulled back up to heaven.

Peter knew that God wasn't telling him to go out and eat lizards or butterflies or vultures. What was he telling him?

It was at that moment that Peter awoke to the sound of knocking. He was about to understand what the dream had meant.

Downstairs were three men sent by an officer named Cornelius. Although Cornelius was Roman, he and his family all believed in God. He was a good man and tried to live a good life. He tried to help the poor, and he spent time praying to God—and God had answered! God had told him to have Peter brought to his house.

As soon as Peter saw that the three men at the door were Gentiles, he invited them in, for now he understood his vision. The very next day he did as they asked and went with them to Cornelius' house in Caesarea, where Cornelius' friends and family had gathered.

Peter looked around. These people were Gentiles, but they were all ready to listen to what he had to say about Jesus. They were no different from the Jews, no less worthy—no less "clean"! For it is sin which makes a person unclean, and when Jesus died on the cross he cleansed everything! God wanted his message to be passed on to the Gentiles just as much as to the Jews. He wanted to give his love to them too.

"God doesn't show favouritism," Peter told his eager listeners. "He doesn't care if you are a Jew or a Gentile. He will welcome anyone who believes in him and tries to follow his laws."

While he was talking about Jesus, the Holy Spirit came. God had given the Gentiles the same gift that he had given to Jesus' special disciples. God's message is for all the people of the world, not just for Jews. That is what Peter's vision had meant!

God doesn't look at the outside of people—he doesn't care about the colour of their skin or what country they come from. He looks at what is in our heart, and his love is for every single person in the world.

Spreading the Good News

The apostles dedicated their lives to spreading the good news—that in trusting God's grace to save us through his Son, Jesus, our sins are forgiven and we are promised an everlasting home in heaven.

Although Paul (Saul usually went by his Roman name these days) was not one of the original twelve apostles, he travelled far and wide as a missionary, travelling to different people in different lands, to pass on the wonderful message about Christ. He spoke to everyone, not just the Jews, just as God had commanded. Sometimes he travelled on his own, sometimes he travelled with friends. Sometimes they were welcomed, sometimes they were not! Either way, he had many strange adventures on his journeys.

Once, some people in a place called Lystra (in modern-day Turkey) decided that when Paul and his friend Barnabas healed a lame man, they must be gods! They wanted to offer them sacrifices and put wreaths around their necks! Barnabas and Paul had a hard job explaining that they were ordinary men and trying to tell them about God!

Later, the people of Lystra turned against Paul because they had been told lies about him by some bad people. They were so angry that they tried to stone him to death and dumped his body outside the city walls. But God hadn't finished with Paul yet—he just picked himself up, brushed himself down, and went back to preach as if nothing had happened!

Then there was the time that Paul and his friend Silas healed a slave girl in Philippi who had been ranting and raving like a mad thing because she had been possessed by an evil spirit. You would have thought that the slave girl's owners would have been happy that the poor girl was back to normal, but instead they were furious. You see, when she had been possessed by the spirit, she had been able to foretell the future, and her owners had made a whole pile of money out of her predictions! Now she had nothing to say, and the money had dried up!

They had Paul and Silas dragged before the city magistrates. The crowd joined in the attack, and Paul and Silas were whipped and beaten and thrown into prison, with their feet locked in stocks.

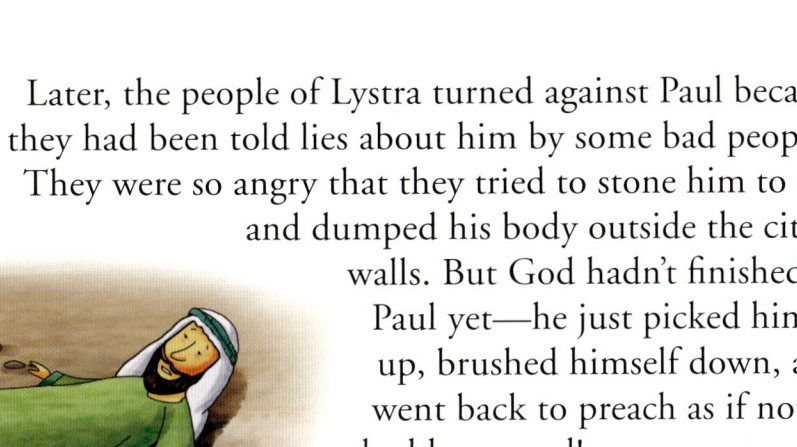

It was midnight. Paul and Silas were lying in the stocks. The chains were tight and the wood was heavy, but they didn't despair. Instead, they were praying and singing hymns. The other prisoners could hardly believe their ears. The usual sounds in prison were of groaning and weeping—not singing!

Suddenly a violent earthquake shook the prison, the cell doors flew open, and everyone's chains came loose! The jailor was more terrified than anyone. He knew that his prisoners would escape and he would get into big trouble, but Paul told him that they wouldn't run away. When the jailor had calmed down enough to listen to him, he invited Paul and Silas back to his own house because he wanted to learn about Jesus, and he wanted his family to learn about him too. They became Christians that very night!

Lots of other strange and wonderful things happened to Paul, but as time went on, he knew it was time for him to return to Jerusalem. He wanted to help the Christians there.

His friends thought he was crazy. "You can't go back to Jerusalem," they protested. "As soon as you enter the city you'll be thrown into prison—or worse! Please don't go!" they pleaded, as he got ready to board a ship heading back to Jerusalem.

But Paul shook his head sadly. "Please don't try to change my mind. This is what I have to do. I'm ready not only to be put in chains for Jesus, but to die for him."

Even though he knew in his heart that hardship and suffering were ahead of him, Paul would go wherever God wanted him to go. Paul's friends wept as he sailed away. They knew that they would never see him again.

Paul travelled to Jerusalem, and sure enough, just as his friends had feared, he was arrested and thrown into jail. The trouble was, no one really knew what to do with him. He hadn't actually broken any laws! But time passed and still he was in prison. In the end he demanded to be seen by Emperor Caesar himself in Rome—all Roman citizens had that right. And so he found himself on board a ship yet again.

Shipwrecked!

Paul was travelling to Rome aboard a ship. To start with, the voyage wasn't unpleasant—Julius, the Roman centurion in charge, was kind to Paul, and some of Paul's friends were on board with him. But bad weather and stops delayed their voyage, and the stormy season was upon them all too soon and forced them to take shelter in a harbour. It really wasn't the right time of year to be sailing, and Paul tried to warn the captain that if they carried on, they would be heading for trouble. But the captain ignored his advice, and the ship set sail.

Soon they found themselves in the middle of a dreadful storm. For days the ship was at the mercy of the angry sea, dragged along by the towering waves and fierce winds. The terrified crew began throwing first the cargo and then anything that they didn't absolutely need over the side to try to save the ship, but it didn't help, and after several days passed without sight of the sun or stars, all hope seemed lost. What else could they do?

Everyone was sitting around glumly, feeling sorry for themselves and certain that they were going to end up at the bottom of the murky ocean. But then Paul spoke up. "I wish you had listened to me when I warned you that this would happen, but even so, there's no point in giving up hope like this. You need to be brave. Everything is going to work out—God has promised that we will all reach land alive. Only the ship will be lost. So cheer up and put your faith in God as I do. It's going to be alright—I promise!"

After two whole weeks at the mercy of the storm, the sailors sensed that they were approaching land, but they were scared that they would be dashed upon the jagged rocks. Some of the sailors tried to leave in one of the lifeboats, but Paul told the captain and Julius that everyone had to stay with the ship to be saved, so they cut the ropes that held the lifeboat and let it drift away.

Paul also made sure that everyone had something to eat. For two whole weeks they had all been too terrified to think about food, but he knew that they had to keep their strength up.

As the sun began to peek over the horizon, a beach finally came into sight. Everyone was so excited! But just as things seemed to be looking up at last, suddenly the ship struck a sandbar. The bow stuck fast, and the ship began to be broken to pieces by the surf!

The soldiers were worried that some of the prisoners might swim away and escape, so they were planning to kill them, but Julius stopped them. He ordered everyone who could swim to make for land, and told those who could not swim to cling to pieces of the broken ship and float ashore.

There were two hundred and seventy-six people on board that ship, and every last one of them reached the shore safely—just as God had promised!

Even when things seem impossible, even when we feel like giving up hope, God can always help us to weather the storm.

Letters of Love

In the end, Paul did finally reach Rome, and while he waited for his case to be heard by the emperor, he was allowed to live by himself, with a soldier to guard him. He couldn't go out, but he could have visitors, and so he was able to carry on spreading the message.

Paul was also a wonderful letter writer. People don't write so many letters nowadays. We pick up the phone and call someone, or maybe drop them an email or a quick text. But Paul couldn't do any of those things! And he couldn't get to see all of his friends. So instead, he wrote letters—wonderful letters of advice and encouragement and love.

Often the friends he was writing to were brand-new Christians whom he had met during his travels. Paul tried to encourage and help them in their important work—they were trying to set up new churches in their towns and cities, and sometimes they had problems. Paul told them that if times seemed hard, they should not give up.

"Whatever hardships and suffering you are feeling now will be more than made up for in heaven!" he wrote. "And remember, often it is our suffering that helps us to get stronger in our faith, so keep your eyes on heaven and rejoice in the Lord!"

He told them to remember that it is faith in Jesus that will save us—"Don't get hung up on obeying lots of little laws," he said. "That isn't the way to get close to God. We can never obey enough laws to be truly good, so we can't be saved by being good, but we can be saved by believing in Jesus. Don't be slaves to the law—Jesus has set us all free, so stay free!"

Paul's words are as useful and important today as they were when he wrote them.

Corinth was a busy sea port, and all kinds of people lived there, doing all sorts of different things. Paul didn't want the people in the new church there to argue amongst themselves about who was the most important or who served God best.

"You're all important!" Paul wrote. "Maybe you can speak in lots of different languages so that you can tell lots of people about God's message. But that doesn't make you more important than someone who can heal people who are sick. And how about the person who has a real gift for teaching? You all need to work together—as a team.

"Or think about it like this—you are all like different parts of one body. Are the arms more important than the mouth? Or the head than the feet? Have you ever tried to stand on your head all day? I wouldn't recommend it! Even those parts of the body that don't seem to have such a big role, or seem weaker, are just as important."

Paul was saying that we should all respect and take care of one another and work together without quarrelling. God has given us all different gifts, different skills and talents. So let's not get big-headed when there's something that we can do well—especially when everything we have is a gift from God in the first place! It doesn't make us better than anyone else. No, instead let's concentrate on using God's gifts to do his work and to help those around us. Each and every one of us is a precious part of the body of Christ—let's all work together!

For Paul, nothing was more important than love—love for God, love for Jesus, and love for one another. Paul told the Corinthians, "If I could speak every single language in the world, even if I could talk with angels, but I didn't love others, I would be no more than a noisy gong or a clanging cymbal. If I had the gift of prophecy, or knowledge, or such great faith that I could move mountains, it would mean nothing if I didn't have love. I could give every last thing that I owned to the poor and suffer great hardship, but it would all mean nothing if I didn't feel love for the people I was doing it for.

"Love is patient and kind. It isn't jealous, boastful, proud or rude. It doesn't insist on having its own way, or become cross, or want revenge, or feel happy when someone else fails. Love protects, and trusts, and hopes. It is steady and true, and it never, ever gives up. Three things will last forever—faith, hope, and love—and the greatest of these is love."

Love gives meaning to everything!

Put on God's Armour!

Ephesus was a bustling port city in the Roman province of Asia Minor, which today is Turkey. It was an important trade city, and Paul had set up the church there. It had been a wicked city with many bad people in it before Paul had come to tell them about Jesus, but through God's kindness it had been saved.

Paul sent its people some wonderful words of encouragement: "Be strong in the Lord. Our real enemies aren't made of flesh and blood—your real battle is against the devil's clever tricks, and to fight that battle you need to put on every piece of God's armour to be prepared.

"Then you can stand your ground confidently, with the belt of truth round your waist and the breastplate of righteousness on your chest. Let your feet be fitted with the readiness that comes from the gospel of peace, and take up the shield of faith. Put on the helmet of salvation and take hold of the sword of the Spirit—the word of God."

What a wonderful image! If we hold on to the truth that the Bible tells us, then we are well prepared to face Satan, the 'father of lies'. If we always choose to do what God says is right, then Satan can't harm us. If we feel ready and at peace because we are assured of God's love for us, then we can stand firm and ready, whatever is coming at us. If we have faith in God, then our faith will protect us from seeds of doubt. Jesus came to earth to save us, and accepting this is our ultimate source of protection. All these things help defend us. Paul suggests only one weapon of attack—but it is the Bible, and that is more than enough, for it is the Word of God!

God's Word and God's love are our protection against all that life can throw at us—they truly are our armour. So let's put on all of God's armour, every last piece, and prepare to do battle!

God is Love

Other writers also had inspiring words to say about faith.

The apostle James wrote, "What good is it to say you have faith if you don't show it by what you do? Words aren't enough, and faith isn't enough—not unless good things come of it."

Peter went on to say, "You face hardship and suffering—but don't despair! Instead, be glad, for these trials make you partners with Christ in his suffering. They will test your faith as fire tests and purifies gold. And remember that there is wonderful joy ahead! Don't be disheartened if it seems a long time in coming—God is being patient, for he wants everyone to repent. But the day of the Lord will come unexpectedly, so be prepared!"

The apostle John wrote, "God is love. He loves us so much that we are called children of God! He showed how much he loved us by sending his one and only Son into the world so that we might have eternal life through him. Since he loved us that much, let us make sure that we love one another so that God can live in us and we can live in God. And as we live in God, our love will grow more perfect, and when the day of judgement comes we will not have to fear anything.

"Perfect love drives out all fear! We love one another because he loved us first. All love comes from God!"

"I'm Coming Soon!"

The very last book of the Bible is Revelation. Many believe it was written by the disciple John. The author had an amazing vision to pass on: He had seen the Son of Man, with hair as white as snow, eyes like blazing fire and a voice like rushing water. The Lord wanted John to send a message to the churches that had been set up across the land, to correct and encourage them.

But that wasn't all. John was also sent a vision of the future . . .

In his vision, John finds himself before the Throne of God and the heavenly court. He sees a scroll with seven seals in the right hand of God, which could only be opened by the Lamb of God, by Jesus himself. And when those seals are opened, dreadful things happen to the world—John sees famine and plague, rivers of blood and terrible beasts—but however bad things get, God's beloved children are kept safe, and in the end, everything evil will be destroyed and God's Kingdom will reign.

John wrote, "Then I saw a new heaven and earth, and I saw the Holy City coming down out of heaven like a beautiful bride. I heard a loud voice speaking from the throne: 'Now God's home is with his people! He will live with them. They shall be his people, and he will be their God. There will be no more death, no more grief, or crying, or pain. He will make all things new! For he is the first and the last, the beginning and the end.'

"And I was shown the Holy City, shining with the glory of God. It had a great high wall with twelve gates and twelve angels in charge of them. The city doesn't need a temple, because God and Christ will be there; it doesn't need the sun or the moon, because the glory of God shines on it, and the Lamb is its lamp. The gates will never be closed, because there will be no night there. And those whose names are written in the Lamb's Book of Life will enter.

"'Listen!' says Jesus. 'I'm coming soon!'

"Let it be so! Come, Lord Jesus, come soon!"

Nobody knows when Jesus is coming—but we know that he definitely is coming! Let's be ready for him, and let's say, just like John did, so many years ago,

"Come, Lord Jesus, come soon!"